THE CAR
AND CITY
THE

24 Steps to Safe Streets and Healthy Communities

Alan Thein Durning

With research assistance by
Beth Callister
Christopher Crowther
Lisa Valdez

NEW Report No. 3
April 1996

Northwest Environment Watch
Seattle, Washington

NEW thanks Meeky Blizzard, Todd Litman, Gussie McRoberts, Terry and Willy Moore, Gordon Price, and Preston Schiller for their cooperation; reviewers Todd Litman and Clifford Cobb for their suggestions; interns Michael Aaron, Aaron Best, Sean Bowles, Sara Jo Breslow, Peter Carlin, Angela Haws, Chandra Shah, and Michael Wewer (who also provided the cover photograph) for their dedicated assistance; and, for their support, volunteers Bill Berg, Monica Bertucci, Mick Braddick, Alycia Braga, Ian Burke, Ed Chadd, Jeff Clark, Susan Clark, Sacha Crittenden, Randy Dill, Jean and Marvin Durning, Sandra Blair Hernsaw, Kevin Klipstein, Norman Kunkel, Wendy Lawrence, Rob Linehan, Flo Lipton, Hollie Lund, Lyn McCollum, Maura McLaughlin, Maria Miller, Emi Nagata, Albert Paulding, Anna Maria Pedroso, Sandy Pernitz, Loretta Pickerell, Don Read, Marilyn Roy, Julene Schlack, Stephanie Smith, Alyson Stage, Scott Stevens, Steve Swope, and Janet Wilson. Design and layout by Visible Images. Edited by Linda Starke and Ellen Chu. Additional research by Todd Litman. The author thanks his entire clan for helping him to meet yet another unreasonable deadline.

Financial support for this report was provided by the Nathan Cummings Foundation and by contributors to Northwest Environment Watch. These include approximately 1,000 individuals and the Bullitt Foundation, Ford Foundation, William and Flora Hewlett Foundation, Global Environment Project Institute, Henry P. Kendall Foundation, Merck Family Fund, Surdna Foundation, an anonymous Canadian foundation, and the Tortuga Foundation. Views expressed are the author's and do not necessarily represent those of Northwest Environment Watch or its directors, officers, staff, or funding organizations. Northwest Environment Watch is a 501(c)(3) tax-exempt organization governed by a board of directors composed of Spencer B. Beebe of Portland; Lester R. Brown of Washington, D.C.; Sandi Chamberlain of Victoria, B.C.; Alan Thein Durning of Seattle; Jane Lubchenco of Corvallis, OR; Tyree Scott of Seattle; and Rosita Worl of Juneau.

Excerpts from this report may be printed in periodicals with written permission from Northwest Environment Watch, 1402 Third Avenue, Suite 1127, Seattle, WA 98101-2118; tel: (206)447-1880; fax: (206)447-2270; e-mail: nwwatch@igc.apc.org.

This book was printed in Vancouver, B.C., using vegetable-based ink and recycled paper. Text: 100 percent postconsumer waste, whitened with hydrogen peroxide and not de-inked in the recycling process. Cover: 10 percent de-inked postconsumer waste, and 40 percent preconsumer waste, whitened without chlorine.

Copyright © 1996 by Northwest Environment Watch
ISBN 1-886093-03-2

TABLE OF CONTENTS

PROLOGUE

THE STAKES

Cars are among the most useful inventions of the past century. They provide private, convenient, door-to-door transportation on demand. They let you go when you want to go, make the stops you want to make, and ride in the company you choose.

Cities are among the most useful developments of all time. They give you access to the diverse talents of hundreds of thousands of people. They let you choose from a richness of economic, educational, cultural, and recreational offerings. They are, in a word, civilized.

This book is about the relationship between these two inventions—the car and the city. It argues that, as wonderful as each is, the two do not always mix well. Specifically, the sheer proliferation of cars is damaging the viability of cities, and only greater attention to the latter will allow the former to work as they should. This book is a call for resurgent cities—cities that improve our lives and, as a little-noticed side effect, lessen our dependence on cars. If we reshape the spaces in which cars operate and overhaul the ways we pay for driving, we will get what we want from cars, and it will cost less. We will also go a long way toward fixing some of the most intractable problems afflicting our communities, economy, and environment.

So, while The Car and the City addresses transportation policy and urban planning, it is also about the defining challenges of this generation: breathing new life into our neighborhoods, revitalizing democracy, and making the public realm safe again. It is about making economies thrive, rooting out a public health menace that kills more people than firearms or illicit drugs, and bridging the widening gaps that divide classes and races. It is about strengthening national security, averting catastrophic climate change, and protecting the vanishing remnants of native wildlands. And it is about conserving that most precious of nonrenewable resources—our own time.

The Car and the City is about all these things because, for North America, the increasingly imbalanced relationship between the car and the city is a crux issue—a problem that lurks unattended behind scores of others. Painful as it is, we must face squarely the fact that unless North Americans can rearrange the furniture of their cities, neither cars nor cities nor North American societies in general will function terribly well.

The book is addressed to all North Americans, but it focuses on the Pacific Northwest, a region that serves as both microcosm and test case. In ecological terms, the Pacific Northwest encompasses the watersheds of rivers that enter the Pacific through the temperate rain forests of North America. It stretches from Prince William Sound in Alaska—where the Trans-Alaska Pipeline fills tankers with fuel for Northwest cars—all the way to the Russian River, north of San Francisco Bay. It extends east to headwaters as far inland as the continental divide in Montana. The most ecologically intact part of the industrial world, this biological zone includes British Columbia, Idaho, Oregon, and Washington, and parts of Alaska, Montana, and California (see map inside front cover). Metropolitan Portland, Seattle, and Vancouver are home to the bulk of the region's 14 million inhabitants, with smaller concentrations in Boise, Victoria, and Spokane.[1]

The Pacific Northwest exemplifies all the dimensions of the existing, dysfunctional relationship between cars and cities. Yet it also possesses a wealth of ingenious solutions. Thousands of citizens are quietly but radically changing their cities, making their region a laboratory for the reinvention of urban life—and a proving ground of international significance. They have disproved the common lament that the sprawling strip developments that came with the automobile are inevitable. They have demonstrated that a great deal can be done to restore cities. They have showed that urban revitalization comes in small steps that have immediate benefits, and that those steps solve many problems at once. What is still unclear is whether enough people will join them in time to make the Northwest a sustainable, viable region. **①** **Read this book on the bus.**

SOLUTIONS

THE CITY

The Honourable Gordon Price, a conservative member of the Vancouver City Council, is in the middle of the street in his neighborhood—the West End—on a wet winter Saturday, greeting some passersby. For a politician, this is not unusual. What is different is that Gordon is not in an automobile: he does not own one. Gordon's peculiarity reflects that of the neighborhood—a tree-lined square mile of apartments, condominiums, offices, and shops between downtown Vancouver and Stanley Park.[2]

"We're standing in the middle of the street," he says, "in the middle of the highest-density residential area in western Canada, and we're not even thinking about traffic." The narrow road—lined with parked cars, leafy trees and shrubs, wide sidewalks, and closely set buildings both tall and short—is empty of moving autos but full of people on foot.

"When I am walking or jogging in the West End, I usually count ten pedestrians for every moving car," notes Gordon. And this ratio explains why he contends that Vancouver's West End, once reviled as a concrete jungle, is "one of the only real answers to the quandary of creating a sustainable and environmentally sound way of life."

Automobiles' private benefits are enormous and well understood. Yet their abundance makes them the source of a disturbing share of social problems. They are the proximate cause of more environmental harm than any other artifact of everyday life on the continent.

Traffic accidents kill more northwesterners each year than gun-shot wounds or drug abuse do: almost 2,000 people in the region died—and 168,000 were injured—in car wrecks in 1993 alone. Traffic deaths move in a mirror image of gasoline prices: when fuel gets cheaper, so does life. The young are especially endangered. Traffic accidents are the leading cause of death among Americans aged ten to twenty-four, and five- to fifteen-year-olds are the age group most likely to be run over by motor vehicles while bicycling. Those older than sixty-five are not exempt from the carnage: they account for the overwhelming share of pedestrians killed by cars.[3]

Cars kill or injure thousands more northwesterners each year without ever touching them: air pollution from motor vehicles—and from the industries that build, fuel, repair, and support them—causes respiratory diseases and lung cancer. In Vancouver, hospital admissions increase on days of bad pollution. Motor vehicles are the single largest source of air pollution in the region. In Washington, road vehicles release 55 percent of all air pollution; in greater Vancouver, they release two-thirds.[4]

"Cars are far cleaner than they used to be," Gordon Price notes, but they remain heavy polluters. And they are the leading cause of climate-changing greenhouse gas emissions. Each car annually emits its own weight in carbon in the form of carbon dioxide—the principal greenhouse gas. Motor fuel combustion accounted for 45 percent of fossil fuel–derived carbon dioxide emitted in the region in 1993, and fuel consumption has since increased.[5]

To grasp the full magnitude of automobiles' downside, add the damage they cause to bodies of water through crankcase drips, oil spills, and the great wash of toxic crud running off roads, driveways, and parking lots. Add the billions of dollars of income drained from the regional economy to pay for its two largest imports: vehicles and oil. Add the crops stunted by air pollution on farms

near cities—losses valued annually at more than $10 million. Add
the fragmentation of every type of wildlife habitat caused by lac-
ing the region with 220,000 miles of public streets and highways.[6]

"Transportation," says Gordon, standing under a row of street
trees on a West End sidewalk, "is a means, not an end. The end is
access." People want to have access to things—services, locations,
facilities. They want to stop at the health club, pick up some groceries, drop by a friend's, and still get home from work at a reason-
able hour. Most of North America has sought to provide this
access through greater mobility; the West End has provided it
through greater proximity.

Access through mobility has involved incredible numbers of cars.
In 1994, there were nearly 11 million motor vehicles in British
Columbia, Idaho, Oregon, and Washington. The motor vehicle
fleet was growing faster than the economy and almost twice as fast
as population. Indeed, it was steadily gaining on the human population; there were four vehicles for every five people. Vehicles
already outnumbered licensed drivers by the late 1960s. If every
driver in the Northwest today took to the roads at the same time,
a million cars would still be parked.[7]

After 1983, driving increased even faster than the number of
autos. Vehicles in Idaho, Oregon, and Washington covered eleven
miles per person a day in 1957; by 1993, the figure was twenty-
five miles per person a day. In part, people were driving farther
each time they got in their cars, but most of the increase was due
to people getting in their cars more often. They were driving on
90 percent of the trips they took. That share had been rising for
decades at the expense of trains, bicycles, buses, and travel by foot.
And the reason for this shift was sprawl. The share of people in
Idaho, Oregon, and Washington who live in suburbs has risen from
just 7 percent in 1950 to 30 percent in 1990 (see Figure 1.)

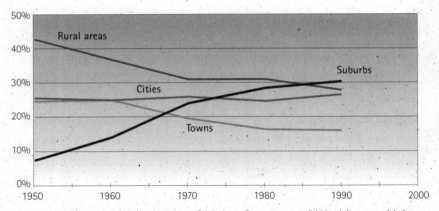

Figure 1. Shares of Population of Idaho, Oregon, and Washington Living in Cities, Suburbs, Towns, and Rural Areas, 1950–1990
More Northwesterners live in suburbs than in cities, towns, or rural areas.
Sources: See endnote 8.

Suburbs overtook towns in population in the 1960s. They passed cities in the 1970s and exceeded rural areas in the 1980s. In Washington, 70 percent of the residences put up between 1960 and 1990 were on the urban fringe.[8]

This kind of urban form was made possible by the automobile; now, it has made the automobile indispensable. People who live in sprawl lack alternatives: people in typical households in northwestern suburbs own one car per driver and get in their cars ten times a day. Per person, suburban dwellers drive three times as far as those who live in pedestrian-friendly urban neighborhoods such as the West End. They are, in transportation lingo, "auto dependent."[9]

Gordon Price's concern is not to fight cars but to fight auto dependence. If he had a car, his bumper sticker would probably read, "Sprawl is the problem. Cities are the solution."

The West End is an eclectic, urbane, polished, somewhat upscale enclave of high-rise and low-rise buildings. To the eye, there is nothing stereotypically "environmental" about it. It is simply a place where things are close enough together that rubber soles transport people better than steel-belted radials do.

Gordon answers most questions about automobiles by talking about the minutiae of architecture and urban design. Access through proximity succeeds, or fails, he argues, in the details of design—the sizes and arrangements of buildings, lots, streets, sidewalks, alleys, crosswalks, parking facilities, parks, and other amenities. Good design, Gordon contends, can create a public realm that is safe, inviting, and conducive to community; bad design creates a menacing and sterile public realm.

Gordon levels his umbrella toward an intersection: "You need a grid system of streets open for pedestrians and bikes, but you must put in diverters now and again to slow cars. Then you green the diverters." **2** **Make streets in a grid. Put in diverters.** A raised concrete planter cuts the intersection diagonally; it is landscaped with trees and shrubs. A traditional street grid broken with these diverters provides smoother movement of traffic—foot, bicycle, and even car—than the sprawl model of cul-de-sacs, feeder roads, connector roads, and highway.

With his umbrella measuring the length of the block, Gordon continues, "Small blocks and narrow lots make walking more interesting." They create a diverse but intimate ambience for foot travellers. **3** **Lay out small blocks with small lots.**

"Narrow streets also slow traffic," Gordon says, because drivers tend to adjust their velocity based on available road space, not posted speed limits. Therefore, motorists who drive the speed limit on city streets—twenty-five miles per hour unless otherwise posted in the U.S. Northwest and fifty kilometers per hour in B.C.— often end up with a string of tailgaters behind them.[10]

Pointing to the curb lane, Gordon says, "Parked cars make pedestrians feel guarded against traffic," which is critical to encouraging walking. To further encourage walking, Gordon says, it is important to have a row of "street trees and grass, then the sidewalk, then landscaping, then buildings" to surround the pedestrian with greenery. **④ Surround the sidewalk with greenery.**

He gestures at the buildings, apartment structures of every size sitting close to the street. "Small setbacks give human scale." Buildings far from the street create yawning, empty spaces that walkers find unwelcoming.

Gordon points at the ample, unshaded ground-floor windows on most of the buildings, "Eyes toward the street give safety." Cohesive neighborhoods full of concerned neighbors and pedestrians, backed by a speedy police force, have proved again and again to be the best defense against lawlessness.[11]

He points out a high-rise tower emerging from a wide, three-story base, "Low-rise facades on the street make high-rises humane for pedestrians, avoiding the concrete canyon effect." From the street, the triple-decker frontage is all you pay attention to: it is modestly scaled and conceals the impersonal bigness of the tower behind.

Perhaps the most surprising thing about the West End is that it completely lacks the boxed-in feeling commonly associated with high density. This openness is achieved in part with lots of cozy "pocket" parks, courtyards, and airy windows, but more of it is due to the attention the government pays to "view lines." Buildings are situated to allow views of greenery, water, and sky. "We try to tend the public realm as carefully as people tend their living rooms," says Gordon.

When all the pieces are assembled, Gordon says, and "you've calmed the traffic down enough, this amazing thing happens. Pedestrians claim the streets, and cars go even slower." International comparisons have showed that the higher a city's average traffic speed, the less walking, bicycling, and transit ridership it will have, and the more gasoline its residents will consume apiece.[12]

Gordon Price is on Denman Street, a commercial avenue where traffic is heavier, and the sidewalks, despite the steady rain, are bursting with people. Some West Enders are sitting under canopies at cafes, others are walking or waiting for buses. It feels like Europe.

Upstairs from some of the shops and bistros are offices; above others are apartments. This mixing of uses—and the close interlacing of the West End's commercial streets with its strictly residential ones—is another ingredient of access through proximity.

⑤ Mix offices, shops, and homes.

In sprawl, zoning codes zealously segregate homes, shops, and workplaces, forbidding apartments above stores, for example, even though this was the main form of affordable housing for generations in North American towns. Mixing stores, homes, and offices creates a more diverse and stable human realm, one where the spheres of life are not geographically fragmented. Mixing uses also moderates the huge fluctuations of population generated by sprawl: residential districts lose their inhabitants by day, commercial districts lose their tenants by night. And automobile numbers are kept high to convey everybody on their daily migrations.

Pausing under one of the many canopies that cover the wide sidewalk, Gordon says, "West End merchants compete for foot traffic by providing pedestrian amenities such as benches and awnings. Elsewhere, merchants compete for car traffic by providing free parking."

"Bike parking is one of our major problems just now," says Gordon, pointing to the two-wheelers locked to every post and fence. The City Engineering Department tallied bicycle trips citywide at nearly 50,000 a day a few years ago, and they have increased since. "Bicycles have been coming out of the woodwork, and the city is just beginning to install enough secure bicycle racks." Vancouver, like Seattle, is also mounting bike racks on buses, just as Amtrak is putting them on the trains connecting Vancouver with Seattle and Portland.[13] **6 Install bike racks.**

Sitting in a restaurant on Denman, Gordon Price looks out through the rain at the public waterfront that rings the city and comes to the crux of the matter. "Of course, none of these details of zoning or design works without a sufficiently concentrated population." Well-designed, mixed-use neighborhoods with few inhabitants per acre do little to lessen auto dependence.

"If we're going to handle growth on a limited land base, one way or another, you're talking about the *D*-word, density. We're in a massive state of denial in the Pacific Northwest about that." Politicians all over the region hear from their constituents that they want lower density and less traffic—which is impossible. Lower density means more traffic, if not on each cul-de-sac, then everywhere else. "Citizens also clamor for better transit, which is another contradiction since transit is hopelessly expensive and inconvenient without sufficient density," says Gordon.

Density—population per acre—is the most important determinant of how dependent citizens are on their automobiles, according to studies of major cities worldwide conducted by Australian researchers Peter Newman and Jeffrey Kenworthy. As population density increases, transportation options multiply and auto dependence lessens, especially as density rises above two thresholds. The first, separating low density from medium density, is at twelve people per acre. Low-density districts—including ninetenths of greater Portland and greater Seattle and more than half of greater Vancouver—have populations that are utterly dependent on autos (see Figure 2).[14]

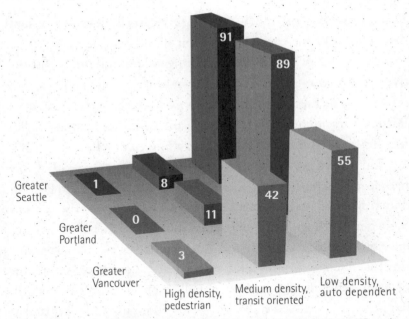

Figure 2. Shares of Metropolitan Population, by Neighborhood Density, Early 1990s

The residents of Vancouver depend far less on the auto than residents of Seattle or Portland.

Sources and definitions: see endnote 14.

In medium-density neighborhoods, including the older in-city neighborhoods of Seattle and Portland and most of Vancouver, bus service becomes an option because there are enough riders to make regular service cost effective. This frees some households from needing multiple cars, so vehicle ownership rates slip and occupancy rates rise: more people ride in each car. In medium-density neighborhoods, total distance driven per person falls, which also lessens per capita gasoline consumption—even though each car's fuel mileage suffers in stop-and-start urban traffic.[15]

As density rises, Newman and Kenworthy found, car traffic slows, but public transit speeds up: as more people take transit, cities invest in faster, dedicated bus lanes and rail transit systems.

Vancouver, like Portland, is building a regional rail transit system. And as density increases, the amount of urban space per resident that must be allocated to roads, parking spaces, and other automotive facilities diminishes. In Vancouver, roughly one-tenth of land is roads alone; the shares in lower-density cities such as Seattle and Portland are higher. Metropolitan Vancouver has roughly half as much road per household as the sprawling city of Kelowna, B.C.[16]

Things just get better above the high-density threshold of forty people per acre. In the Northwest, only Seattle's First Hill and Vancouver's West End and its surrounding neighborhoods have high density. Above this higher threshold, destinations are close enough that bicycling and foot travel flourish, people drive one-third as much as in low-density districts, and as many as one-third of households do not own a car at all. Air pollution falls especially fast because the added walking, biking, and transit trips replace the short, cold-engine car trips that pollute the most per mile.[17]

Transit thrives as well at high densities. West End buses run often enough—roughly once every seven minutes—that no one needs a schedule. And because ridership is high, most buses turn a healthy profit. Indeed, buses in greater Vancouver overall generate half of their operating budgets from fares, compared with less than one-fourth in Seattle and Portland.[18]

The decline in auto dependence at higher densities holds true regardless of income: Poor people in the suburbs drive more than rich people in the city. Rich people in high-density areas take the bus more than poor people on the periphery.[19]

"If we accept that density must increase, how do we do it?" Gordon Price asks. "The city of Vancouver now is emerging as a leader in how to do it." The West End is a case in point. More than a century ago, the West End held the two- and three-story mansions of the well-to-do. By early in the 1900s, these structures had been divided into flats, boarding hotels, and tenements. It became a working-class neighborhood from which laborers could get to their jobs on foot, bicycle, or streetcar. In June 1956, the Vancouver City Council rezoned the area for multifamily residential buildings, and by 1962 a building boom took hold. Towers went up left and right, filling with renters as quickly as they could be completed.[20]

Then the citizens of Vancouver brought construction screeching to a halt. Offended by high-rises, they realigned municipal politics and shut down new construction in most of Vancouver's residential neighborhoods. Of course this move did nothing to stop development. Population was growing, the number of households was growing faster, and demand for additional floor space was growing fastest of all. The building boom was shunted beyond city limits, and the metropolis expanded like a supernova up the Fraser River Valley.

On the city council, Gordon has fought back by helping to approve grandiose development plans for two other areas on the fringe of downtown, plans that will double the residential population of the city's central core. "The West End is full. We have to create new West Ends. The single-family neighborhoods will never let in new development, so we had to encourage building on underused industrial land around downtown." **7 Build new highrise neighborhoods in depressed industrial zones.**

In Seattle, a citizens' group has been calling for creation of something similar, to be known as Seattle Commons: a new walkable neighborhood of 15,000 residents in a zone of parking lots and light-industrial buildings. The Commons would involve the removal of about forty acres of pavement to create a central park stretching from the shores of Lake Union to downtown.[21]

Meanwhile, Gordon has also been instrumental in expanding an ambitious elevated-rail transit system called Skytrain. More important, he has pushed hard and successfully for aggressive development around the stations—miniature West Ends popping up like beads on the strings of rail.[22]

"Living in apartments or condominiums, especially high rises, is not for everyone," Gordon says. "But it is an option in much greater demand than is commonly recognized. Most new apartment and condo buildings within walking distance of downtowns—whether in Vancouver, Seattle, or Portland—fill almost immediately."

Market research conducted for the Puget Sound Regional Council in greater Seattle shows that while three-fourths of people prefer detached houses to higher-density options, most people care more about the quality of the neighborhood and owning their own home than they care about housing type. In the right circumstances, more than 90 percent would trade low-density living for high-density neighborhoods—some would move into high-rises, others into low-rises, town houses, or detached houses on small lots. Where in-city town house and condominium development make homeownership more affordable, for example, buyers are already abundant. Other powerful magnets include good neighborhood schools, a sense of community, local parks and a feeling of openness, good transit service, neighborhood shops, and—most important by far—low crime rates. Indeed, fully one-third of low-density dwellers in greater Seattle would enthusiastically move into a medium- or high-density neighborhood if they felt safe there. Vancouver's West End has all these features. Indeed, violent crime rates in Vancouver are a small fraction of those in the United States.[23] **❽ Fight urban crime.**

Despite the market demand, neighborhoods throw up political barriers to development. Neighborhoods of single-family houses are vehemently opposed to multifamily buildings, especially rental units. In community meetings throughout the region, the words "high-rise" are spit like a curse. Most single-family neighborhoods even object to homeowners renting out excess space in their houses as accessory apartments—"granny flats" or "mother-in-law apartments," as they are sometimes called. In many low-density neighborhoods in the Pacific Northwest, adding two granny flats per block would be enough to push the area into the medium-density population range.[24]

The root of this sentiment, Gordon believes, is "fear of 'the other.'" House owners assume apartment dwellers are poor and a danger to property values. "The problem is that when we hear the word density . . . we think of crime-infested public housing

Location-Efficient Mortgages

A minor modification of mortgage-lending rules written by independent banks and government-sponsored mortgage guarantors, such as the Federal National Mortgage Association (Fannie Mae), could help the affordability of urban housing. These homes are often more expensive than suburban housing because they are close to jobs and city amenities.

Households in urban neighborhoods can often shed a second or third car, however, saving an average of $300 a month for each. Mortgage rules should allow them to spend some of these savings on a more expensive home. Fannie Mae already has a similar program for energy-efficient houses. Buyers of certified efficient houses are allowed to borrow more than buyers of other houses since the saved energy expenses allow higher mortgage payments. **9** **Factor auto dependence into mortgage qualification rules.**

Location-efficient mortgages would help both buyers and existing owners since some of the increased borrowing power would be capitalized in higher property values. This would create an incentive for neighborhoods to improve their "location efficiency" by recruiting shops, workplaces, and other development and by lobbying for better transit service.[25]

projects—vertical slums." What northwesterners ought to think about, Gordon suggests, is the West End. Or Paris, which has three times the density of Seattle. Or Amsterdam, Copenhagen, London, Munich, Rome, Stockholm, or Vienna—all places with vastly higher density than Portland or Vancouver. In these cities, fewer than half of all trips are taken by automobile, not the 90 percent found in Northwest cities.[26]

As dusk falls, Gordon sprints two blocks up Denman, chasing a bus that is headed for one of the new West Ends he has helped create as a member of the city council: Yaletown—a derelict warehouse district half converted to a mixed neighborhood of youth clubs, restaurants, art shops, and condominiums. The streets in the new zone have a raw feeling absent in the West End. "The trees and landscaping will take about ten years to fill out," he laments. "And these buildings are a little too massive and uniform. But every building that's been finished has filled immediately. And when the new neighborhood is done, there'll be another West End's worth of people here."

Then, standing out of the rain under another canopy, Gordon reveals his grand political strategy. "What happens when all these developments are completed? Think about it. The business district will be surrounded by pedestrian neighborhoods. They will become politicized. They won't want high-speed through-traffic in their neighborhoods." They will say "Enough!" to the 175,000 cars that drive into their city each day. They will become a pedestrian voting bloc. **⑩ Surround downtown with pedestrian voters.**

Throughout the Pacific Northwest, people like Gordon Price are working to envelope people and cars in a richer and more varied urban landscape. Block by block, zoning hearing by zoning hearing, they are fighting to refashion their cities, aiming for a future where cars serve communities, not the other way around.

From Portland through Seattle to Vancouver, the Northwest's major cities are engaged in far-reaching planning efforts—all of which are strikingly similar, at least in the vision they paint of the future. According to this new vision, most population growth will concentrate in central cities and in satellite hubs rather than in undifferentiated sprawl. Downtowns will once again be ringed with dense middle-class neighborhoods, with low-income and high-income housing mixed throughout rather than concentrated in pockets.[27]

New development will be mixed use rather than monocultures of residences, shopping palaces, or office parks. Streets will be designed to accommodate pedestrians, bicyclists, buses, and trolleys as well as private cars. Express buses and rail transit will knit the city together internally and connect seamlessly to intercity train stations, bus terminals, and airports. Each transit station will be surrounded by tightly clustered workplaces, shops, and apartment buildings, moving outward to town houses, and finally to detached houses on small lots. Minibuses will circulate from each transit station, further strengthening the sense of community. Telecommuting, teleshopping, and video-conferencing techniques will make mouse-and-modem the preferred vehicle for some trips. And information technology ranging from pocket beepers to the World Wide Web will allow quick trip planning and carpool coordination.[28]

This vision is the officially sanctioned hope at least. Whether it will come to be is another question.

THE PROBLEM

SPRAWL

S prawl has three defining characteristics. It is a lightly populated urban form: there are fewer than twelve people per acre. It is a rigidly compartmentalized urban layout: shops, dwellings, offices, and industries are kept separate, as are different types of each, so apartment buildings and detached single-family houses do not mingle. And it is an urban form with a branching street pattern: small streets begin at cul-de-sacs and feed only into progressively larger streets until they meet high-speed thoroughfares.[29]

What is wrong with sprawl? Four things: it is expensive, dangerous, antienvironmental, and antisocial.

First, expensive: sprawl burdens the economy. In sprawl, everyone has to have his or her own car. On average, that costs $300 a month per car. Americans at the median income work twenty-seven hours a month paying for the thirty-two hours a month they spend driving (and some of the time, they are commuting). True average driving speed works out to seventeen miles per hour—comparable to the thirteen miles per hour traveled by typical bicyclists.

Sprawl requires longer and wider roads, more sewer pipes, more electric and water lines, more television cables, and more storm-water drains. Extending this infrastructure to each new dwelling on the edge of an existing neighborhood—assuming housing is built at urban densities of twelve units per acre—costs about $23,000. In suburban-style tracts with three houses an acre, the cost of infrastructure rises by half. In "exurban" developments—those tucked into the countryside beyond the suburbs—the cost doubles.[30]

Sprawl necessitates more and bigger garages, and more public parking spaces, each built for upward of $1,000 plus whatever the land costs; in parking garages, construction costs are more likely $15,000 per space. Sprawl pushes fire, ambulance, and police services to their limits. It makes trash and recycling collection—and postal delivery—more expensive. It lowers the effectiveness of workers and businesses because it leads to traffic congestion: in the Seattle area, time and fuel lost to traffic jams is estimated to be worth $740 million a year.[31]

The increased frequency of car crashes sprawl leads to puts a huge burden on the economy: the insurance and medical costs incurred from car wrecks, and the wages lost, siphon roughly $8 billion a year from the region's economy. (In fact, crashes are such an economic drain and so many are caused by young drivers and drunk drivers that raising the driving age to eighteen, making transit free for all minors, and stiffening drunk driving laws would likely boost productivity and employment rates.)[32]

Sprawl makes affordable housing difficult to find near workplaces and increases commute times. It reduces the productive rural land base: sprawl around Vancouver comes at the expense of the best farmland in British Columbia; likewise, Portland sprawls into some of Oregon's most fertile land. All these costs drag down the economy, suppressing real incomes.[33]

Taxpayers pick up the tab for billions of dollars of these increased costs because governments subsidize both driving and sprawl with handouts, tax breaks, and uncompensated services. Sprawl is even a losing venture for local governments: a 1993 review of research literature showed that residential development on farmland is usually a drain on government revenue because the increased property taxes and development fees do not cover the extra costs of public services. Even shopping center development is often a revenue loser, counting the extra police and fire service required and the unplanned strip development that tends to follow.[34]

Sprawl's other deleterious effects, from pollution to the deteriorating cohesiveness of communities, also tend to create problems that increase tax burdens. One-third of injuries caused by car crashes in the United States, for example, result in expenditures under federal medical assistance programs, according to the U.S. Department of Transportation.[35]

Sprawl is dangerous. It undermines public safety and makes national security precarious. It makes people drive more, and driving is among the most dangerous things people do. Since 1980, motor vehicles have killed almost 31,000 northwesterners and injured more than 2 million—far more than have died or been injured as a result of violent crime. Tragically, people often flee crime-ridden cities for the perceived safety of the suburbs—only to increase the risks they expose themselves to.[36]

Because of strong psychological reactions to what criminologists call "stranger danger"—the fear of random, malicious acts—people tend to overestimate the risks of crime while dramatically underestimating the risks of driving. Crime rates per capita in Seattle, for example, vary surprisingly little across all types of neighborhoods, and most crimes are committed by acquaintances, not strangers. Still, in the extreme case, the per capita rate of violent crime might be one-tenth as high in a distant suburb—say Issaquah—as in a close-in urban neighborhood—say Queen Anne. Consider, however, that the risk of an injury-causing car crash—already a more serious risk than crime for the Queen Anne dweller—roughly quadruples in Issaquah. It does so because residents of distant suburbs commonly drive three times as much, and twice as fast, as urban dwellers. All told, city dwellers are much safer.[37]

Sprawl is also bad for public safety because it reduces the number of watchful eyes on the street. There is even a possibility that sprawl is related, tangentially, to domestic violence. A national study of violence against children in the United States found that neighborhood cohesiveness—households' sense of belonging to their community—was among the most important defenses against child abuse. And sprawl is designed for privacy, not community. That same failing may be contributing to the emergence of youth gangs in middle-class suburbs. Lasting personal connections with responsible adults, whether parents, ministers, or neighbors, are the best safeguard against destructive influences on adolescents. Yet, as youth-violence specialist Delton Young writes in the *Seattle Post-Intelligencer*, "Everything about the way our suburban towns are built discourages cohesion among families, neighbors, and communities. . . . If we tour through large sections of the Lynnwoods, the Bellevues and the Federal Ways, we might well ask, 'Why wouldn't a kid join a gang, growing up here?'"[38]

This form of development is even bad for national security because it creates auto dependence, and auto dependence translates into oil consumption levels that can only be supplied through large petroleum imports. The Northwest's motor vehicles account for three-fourths of all petroleum consumed in the region. Securing the region's cities therefore requires defense of distant oil fields and supply routes. These include political hot spots like the Middle East. In the 1980s, annual U.S. military budgets were approximately $40 billion higher than they would have been if the Middle East had not been a national security interest.[39]

Sprawl increases pollution and resource consumption. Because it induces so much driving, sprawl is bad for the air, human health, and the climate. Canadian cities such as Vancouver emit twice the greenhouse gases per resident that Amsterdam releases, mostly because of sprawl. And Seattle and Portland emit half again as much per capita as Vancouver.[40]

Sprawl boosts the amount of land, water, and energy required to provide for each inhabitant of an area. Because of sprawl, greater Seattle's developed land area, for example, grew more than twice as fast as its population between 1970 and 1990. By the end of this period, metropolitan Seattle was overtaking nine square miles of woodland, farmland, and other open space each year. In the Vancouver region, sprawl was advancing too, although less than half as quickly, according to data for the mid-1980s.[41]

Overall, in Idaho, Oregon, Washington, and western Montana, the area of developed land grew faster than population in the decade leading up to 1992. Development overtook an acre every nine minutes during this period—nine hundred square miles in total. Sprawl fills wetlands; nearly 70 percent of the tidal wetlands in Puget Sound are lost, mainly to suburban development. It rearranges shorelines, dikes rivers, increases storm-water runoff and sewage overflows, and otherwise alters the chemistry and structure of aquatic habitats.[42]

Sprawl ruins streams: paving and building on just 15 percent of a watershed's surface area—a percentage reached at an extremely low population density—so affects water-flow regimes that it pushes most stream ecosystems out of whack. Diverse forms of insect, fish, and plant life give way to impoverished arrays of weedy, stress-tolerant species. For example, coho salmon—an endangered species in much of their range—are seldom found when impervious cover exceeds 15 percent. In western Washington, some biologists suspect sprawl—and the changes in local water-flow patterns it brings—as a cause of steep declines in certain native frog populations.[43]

Sprawl increases the consumption of water, used to irrigate big lawns and wash multiple cars. It compounds energy consumption for heating: the clustered buildings and apartments common in cities shelter each other from the cold, but detached suburban buildings do not. And sprawl escalates gasoline consumption.[44]

Sprawl erodes civil society—the human glue of democracy. It aggravates social and economic inequality and frays community cohesiveness. Sprawl makes owning a car a necessity of life, which can transform a low income into a poverty income. It also siphons customers away from inner-city groceries, which raises local food prices and again makes poverty more expensive. It draws jobs, investment capital, and tax base from urban to suburban areas. The flight of the successful leaves behind neighborhoods short on role models, local businesses, volunteers for the community center, homeowners, contributors to the PTA, and hope. And these abandoned neighborhoods are prone to succumb to the concomitants of poverty—welfare dependency, teen pregnancy, violence, and school failure. Completing the vicious circle, these in turn speed flight to the suburbs by those who can afford to go.[45]

It is not just the poor who suffer from the inequality of sprawl. It hurts people who are unable to drive, including children and some of the elderly and the handicapped. Sprawl can become a sentence of isolation and immobility for senior citizens. Low-density urban plans, the American Association of Retired Persons writes, "make older persons heavily dependent on automobiles to conduct basic tasks such as grocery shopping or visiting the doctor, even as their desire or ability to drive diminishes." Likewise, kids in sprawl cannot walk or ride their bikes to school or friends' homes because of the traffic and the distance. By isolating children, sprawl turns parents into chauffeurs.[46]

Sprawl saps the sense of civic community—the notion people have that, despite their diversity, they are all in it together. It limits interaction between classes, ages, and races. It arranges people geographically according to their economic standing because apartment buildings, row houses, and detached houses are seldom mixed. This insulates the affluent from fellow citizens who are poor and isolates the poor from the social networks that bind the affluent. Physical segregation wreaks havoc on fellow feeling.[47]

Sprawl is bad for community in the more general sense of neighborliness too. When everyone is driving, there is little chance of striking up casual conversations. Americans now typically spend eight hours a week in their cars. And there is less space where community might blossom: the walkable public realm is swallowed by cars and structures oriented toward them. Roads, parking lots and garages, and other automotive facilities absorb as much as a quarter of urban space in Northwest cities.[48]

The landscape of sprawl does nothing to entice people into the public realm where community might develop. It is designed for consumption at highway speeds. Architectural detail and graphic subtlety—the aesthetic rewards for lingering in public spaces—become irrelevant. All that matters is whether a driver can recognize a place of commerce from far enough away to get into the turn lane. This has the insidious effect of favoring chain stores with distant owners over locally owned businesses with human ties to place; this tendency, in turn, accelerates the concentration—and uprooting—of wealth. Sprawl is also bad for community identity, which is established partly by the shared understanding of unique assets such as historic buildings and squares. These fare poorly when it is so cheap to move to strawberry-tinted office parks out by the freeway.[49]

For all these reasons, sprawl makes the practice of democracy—the formal processes through which communities govern themselves—difficult. Where a sense of community is lacking, democracy devolves into a game of least common denominators. Worse, sprawl puts jurisdictions that cover small parts of a metropolis into active competition with each other for jobs, tax base, and federal funds.[50]

Is sprawl good for anything? It is good for scores of industries, ranging from oil companies and car makers to lube shops and drive-through restaurants. It is good for speculators in real estate. And, because buying influence is a normal cost of business among real estate speculators, it is good for campaign contributions. Real estate interests put up 5 percent of the contributions to state legislative races in Washington from 1990 to 1994—twice as large a share as even the big-spending timber industry. They likely accounted for a much larger share of contributions to candidates for city and county offices, where critical land use decisions are made. And they bankrolled most of the anti–land use planning "takings" legislation and initiatives across the Northwest during 1994 and 1995. Perhaps this influence explains why sprawl continues despite the best efforts of urban planners.[51]

THE ORIGINS

POLITICS

How did the Northwest end up burdened with its present urban design? Some argue that it was the result of millions of people's informed decisions interacting in a free and fair marketplace. To try to change it, they contend, is "social engineering." A look at history suggests otherwise: government policies have been as important as market forces in shaping the urban Northwest.

In the 1890s, two new inventions—electric streetcars and bicycles with inflatable tires—came on the scene in force. Together these allowed the working class—previously the walking class—an unprecedented gain in travel speed. From trudging around town at roughly three miles an hour, they accelerated to about twelve miles an hour. Automobiles in city traffic do not go much faster today. Streetcars gave form to booming Portland, Seattle, and Vancouver, channeling growth along densely built corridors radiating from the town centers. Streetcar neighborhoods from this era remain the most walkable, and in many cases the most sought-after, addresses in the region: the West End of Vancouver, Madison Park and Capitol Hill of Seattle.[52]

Then came the motor car. At first, its effect was narcotic. In the wide-open Northwest, cars sold like hotcakes. They increased in number from essentially nil at the turn of the century to nearly 1 million in 1929 (see Figure 3). The automobile offered individualized mobility at (were it not for traffic) unimaginable speeds.[53]

By the 1920s, local and national governments besieged by auto industry lobbyists were prying up cobblestones, extending and widening streets, installing traffic lights and signs, motorizing police forces, and regulating streetcars that competed for road

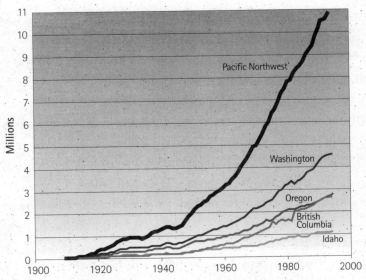

Figure 3. Motor Vehicles, Pacific Northwest, 1900–1994
Growth of vehicle numbers has been rapid.
Sources: see endnote 53.

space. By 1923, all Northwest jurisdictions had enacted motor fuel taxes solely dedicated to financing roadwork. Later, when British Columbia, California, Idaho, and Washington enacted sales taxes to finance the general functions of governments, all but California exempted motor fuels on the spurious basis that motor fuels were already taxed.[54] **11 Don't exempt gasoline from retail sales tax.**

When the Depression hit in 1929, the U.S. government began pumping billions of dollars into road construction, battling a slack economy with miles of asphalt. Similarly, the Federal Housing Authority (FHA) began to shovel money into construction. It favored the reliably uniform new houses going up outside of town. Row houses, duplexes, and anything else where people shared walls had a harder time qualifying for FHA loans.[55]

Meanwhile, entire neighborhoods of old city houses, increasingly occupied by people with African or Asian ancestors, were disqualified outright. The practice was called redlining. And it was only the latest flavor of discrimination used to segregate people by their skin color. In the Central District of Seattle, the Northwest's largest African-American neighborhood, redlining was one in a series of kinds of housing bias. In the 1920s, city elders wrote restrictions into homebuyers' deeds in white neighborhoods forbidding them from selling to "undesirables." In the 1940s, these "restrictive covenants" were replaced by "voluntary agreements." In the 1960s, these too were banned, but private banks and insurance companies had picked up redlining where the FHA had left off. The Central District was deemed a bad risk: no loans, and no homeowner's insurance.[56]

Car numbers in the Northwest hardly grew between 1929 and the end of World War II, but New Deal housing and road building policies had an enormous impact on the U.S. Northwest after the war. Wartime industries and military bases oriented toward the Pacific had brought hundreds of thousands of people to the region. Many of them stayed afterward, using FHA and new Veterans Administration loans to buy cheap houses in the suburbs. In the decade after World War II, roughly half of U.S. home sales were financed through these government-insured mortgages.[57]

A provision in the federal income tax code grew to be an even more powerful stimulant to sprawl than home financing. The interest on home mortgages became tax-deductible. Every dime an owner paid to a bank in interest on a home loan could be subtracted from his or her income before calculating the taxes due. As personal income tax grew to become the principal source of federal money, the incentive to buy bigger, more expensive houses—which often meant suburban mansions—increased. This loophole is one of the largest handouts in the U.S. tax code, and a huge indirect subsidy to sprawl.[58] **(12) Eliminate the mortgage interest deduction.**

In the postwar boom years, rapid growth in personal income, combined with two additional stimulants to sprawl, raised car numbers in the Northwest from barely more than 1 million at war's end to nearly 6 million on the eve of the oil embargo in 1973.

The first stimulant was decentralized: beginning in the 1950s, civil engineers began packaging generic zoning and urban planning codes and distributing them to jurisdictions across the continent, which passed them into law. Sadly, the consequence was that the same suburbs began to appear everywhere: gas station–sized residential lots impossible to connect into walkable communities; off-street parking requirements that ensured most new retail buildings would be islands in seas of pavement; highway designs that consigned acres of open space to clover-leaf interchanges and yawning medians, along with mathematical models that "proved" the necessity of more expressway lanes than could possibly be built; and oversized neighborhood streets that swirled and twirled through curlicues, flourishes, and all the forms of the rococo masters.[59]

The second tonic to sprawl was highly centralized. In 1956, Congress approved construction of a national system of interstate highways. The interstates would form a network of divided, limited-access speedways of four or more lanes that would tie the country together, lubricate commerce, open the countryside, and let all Americans experience the convenience, exhilaration, and "freedom" of gunning their V8s. Freeways were a giant public works project, arguably larger than anything created by the New Deal. The federal funds, covering 90 percent of the tab, were spread among almost every congressional district in the country.[60]

Considering the gargantuan scale of the endeavor, debate over the interstate highway act was paltry. In Washington State, there was a brief effort to leave space for a rail transit line in the middle of the planned Interstate 5, but auto interests quickly squelched such talk. Indeed, few had anything bad to say about the freeways while they were being built, because nobody had any idea what they would do to cities.[61]

It was almost too late before some northwesterners realized that putting a freeway through your city to improve transportation is like putting a hole through your heart to improve circulation. Urban freeways sucked people, money, and vitality out of town; as the interstates were built, the cities deteriorated. The interstates were a monstrous, taxpayer-funded sprawl accelerator that turned the midcentury move to the suburbs into the largest migration in U.S. history. Freeways destroyed urban retailing by giving birth, first in Seattle, to the shopping mall—a saccharine imitation of Main Street that spread from one freeway interchange to the next like an infectious disease. (By the late 1980s, the Northwest's shopping centers outnumbered high schools, and a new breed of retailers called superstores—discount establishments the size of airplane hangars—had successfully implanted themselves alongside other freeways.)[62]

The 1970s were a period of uncertainty for the car. It was being criticized for the first time for its environmental faults even while the price of its fuel was gyrating wildly. After the Soviet invasion of Afghanistan, President Carter declared that any attempt by a foreign power to consolidate control over Middle Eastern oil fields would be taken as an act of trespass against the United States. The Pentagon began to spend tens of billions of dollars each year keeping ready to fight wars in faraway deserts. Yet cheap imported vehicles and a demographic revolution were pushing auto numbers up more quickly than ever before or since.[63]

Middle-class women joined their working-class sisters in the labor force and, given the already dispersed form of Northwest cities, the change meant second cars for millions of families. From 1973 to 1980, the car population rose from less than 6 million to almost 8 million. During this time, government regulations were making cars cleaner and more fuel efficient. When fuel prices finally dropped in the mid-eighties, the real cost per mile of fueling an automobile was lower than ever before, setting the stage for even more driving.

In the 1980s, President Reagan deregulated the savings and loan industry, freeing hundreds of thrift institutions to invest in exurban office parks and strip malls. This act gave another subsidy to sprawl since the federal government was underwriting the loans through its deposit insurance. In the mid-1980s, new shopping centers were opening nationwide at the rate of one every four hours. Many were white elephants that quickly failed, pulling down scores of thrifts. The debts—projected to reach $150 billion by the year 2000—began landing on the U.S. Treasury. Meanwhile, regulators stepped in and auctioned off the exurban commercial and retail space at liquidator prices, undercutting urban buildings that had not benefited from the bail out. Sprawl had again been served and, adjusting to the new requirements of life, the people of the Northwest bought more cars, bringing the total to more than 10 million by 1990.[64]

Then came the 1990s, and a fast-forward replay of the previous two decades: in rapid succession there was an oil war in the Middle East, a flowering of environmental consciousness and support for limits on sprawl and investment in rail transit, and a political pendulum swing to the right. All the while, motor vehicle numbers surged upward, with the speediest growth among fuel-guzzling four-wheel-drive passenger trucks. Speed limits were raised, suppressing the operating efficiency of the region's vehicle fleet and boosting traffic deaths. By 1994, British Columbia, Idaho, Oregon, and Washington together had 11 million motor vehicles for 10 million licensed drivers. They also had roughly 25 million parking spaces—all of them connected by 220,000 miles of public streets and highways, enough to circle the globe nine times.[65]

Was sprawl inevitable? No. Political leaders chose it. Look at the difference in decision making for rail transit and highway construction. The United States, and to a lesser extent Canada, chose to invest in—and subsidize—cars and roads rather than cities and transit. No voters anywhere ever approved the interstate highway system or the state and provincial highways constructed at taxpayer expense. And no amount of local initiative could turn that tide. The voters of greater Seattle, for example, were asked in 1958, 1962, 1968, 1970, 1988, and 1995 whether to rebuild its rail transit system. A majority usually voted "yes," but never by the 60 percent margin required for approval of bond measures. Portland, with different voting rules, finally succeeded in reseeding rail in the 1980s, but on a scale that could hardly compete with the road infrastructure.[66]

Was sprawl inevitable in the Northwest? Look at Portland's example. Downtown Portland is probably the best case of urban planning in the western United States, combining all the elements of successful cityscapes from near and far: small blocks with shop windows and small businesses at street level, narrow streets, crosswalks laid in brick to demarcate the realm of pedestrians, parks, fountains, statues sprinkled throughout, and, above all, a vibrant mixture of uses—offices, stores, and residences—and of classes— rich, middle, and poor. Some of this came about fortuitously, but most of it was won in pitched political battles.[67]

The definitive phase of warfare was probably over the proposed Mount Hood Freeway, a leg of the interstate system that would have bulldozed 1 percent of the city's housing. A grassroots coalition rallied to block the freeway in the late 1960s and early 1970s. By all accounts, it was a contest for the soul of the city, pitting a generation of young turks against the old-guard proponents of progress by civil engineering. The turks prevailed.[68]

Under the leadership of Republican Governor Tom McCall, Oregon then passed the nation's firmest farmland protection and growth management law in 1972, and Portland set about doing the opposite of everyone else—a pattern that has since continued. In the 1970s, when other cities were condemning whole neighborhoods to put in freeways, Portland was demolishing an expressway along the Willamette in favor of a two-mile riverfront park. When other cities were approving scores of downtown parking garages, Portland put a moratorium on downtown parking growth and converted a parking lot into a town square. That quadrangle, Pioneer Courthouse Square, has become the hub of the metropolis.[69]

During the Reagan administration, while other cities were slashing bus service, Portland reinstalled tracks in its streets, breaking ground on a light-rail system called MAX. Wildly popular, MAX has since gained the approval of Oregon voters by lopsided margins each time it has sought additional funds. Portland paid attention to the details: to prevent delays at each stop, for instance, MAX has trackside wheelchair lifts rather than onboard ones. New lines, furthermore, will have low-floor cars, so passengers will not even have to climb steps to board the train. (In 1995, B.C. Transit began adding low-floor buses to its fleet for the same reason.) To further speed the system, Portland dispensed with fare collection. Tickets are sold by vending machines on the platform. To ensure compliance, transit police randomly board trains and write stiff fines to anyone who does not have a valid ticket. All these steps have helped because time is the currency of transportation.[70]

Meanwhile, within its downtown, Portland made buses free, put up shelters at all stops, installed closed-circuit television monitors with up-to-the-minute bus schedules, and took a main arterial back from cars to make a central transit mall. Dedicating the

Make Way for Transit

Slowly but surely, the Northwest is recognizing that for transit to compete with cars, buses must move as quickly as possible through traffic. The symbol of the failure to do so is the common sight of a bus with 60 passengers stuck in a line of cars. Portland has a buses-only street; Seattle has an express tunnel through downtown for commuter buses. But these are just the beginning of what is possible. Some buses in Kitsap County, Washington, have radio transponders that instruct traffic signals to turn green, and Seattle is beginning to test these on some routes. Ideally, buses should never be faced with red lights. Similarly, transit vehicles should have the right of way when merging into traffic from a stop. That principle is now the law in Seattle, but it is unenforced and unknown to most drivers. Experience in Curitiba, Brazil, shows that a network of dedicated bus lanes, low-floor buses, curbside fare collection, and raised boarding platforms works almost as well as a rail transit system, and for a fraction of the cost.[71]

downtown to people on foot, they also largely stopped enforcing jaywalking laws. All the changes made a difference. Between 1970 and 1990, the number of jobs downtown increased by half, the share of downtown workers riding transit rose to more than 40 percent, car traffic entering downtown stabilized, and the air got cleaner.[72]

Outside downtown, Portland was promoting multifamily housing and declaring war on traffic. Earl Blumenaur, public works commissioner from 1986 on, earned himself a reputation as the Earl of Speed Bumps. He had city workers begin installing speed bumps, speed humps, traffic diverters, traffic circles, and street-narrowing curb "bubbles" almost on demand. Said Blumenaur, only the fire department—which does not like to slow its million-dollar trucks for anything—stood between him and speed bumping the entire city. (In 1995, the city of Boise caught speed bump fever from Portland, installing sixty-two in the first half year alone and watching traffic velocity drop by a quarter at each bump.)[73] **13 Calm traffic.**

In 1994, Portland citizens began putting a fleet of 450 brightly painted community bicycles on the streets, quickly inspiring imitators in Salem, Oregon, and Victoria, B.C. The wide-ranging two-wheelers are free to use and left where they fall until someone else needs a ride. The idea is usually said to have come from Europe, but a similar system has been used inside the Boeing Company's giant production facilities around Puget Sound for decades.[74]

Was sprawl inevitable? Compare British Columbia with the American Northwest. British Columbia was less enamored of the automobile. Canada never built an interstate: the country has a quarter as many lane-miles of urban freeway per capita as the United States. British Columbian drivers pay higher taxes on vehicles and fuels than other northwesterners, get no income tax deduction for mortgage interest, and pay more for auto insurance, too. They use a road network two notches less developed than that south of the border. They cannot go quite as fast. Consequently, cities—while still far from compact enough for sustainability—are less sprawled (see Table 1). Vancouver has fewer auto-dependent residents, more multifamily dwellings, more use of transit, fewer cars per person, and less driving per person. In the 1980s, greater Vancouver converted less rural land to urban uses for every additional thousand residents than any other Canadian metropolis. And it was sprawling at one-third the rate of Seattle, despite comparable population growth.[75]

The fate of Interstate 5 illustrates the differences within the region. In Seattle, the freeway cuts a canyon through the heart of the city from north to south, swelling to as many as sixteen lanes and two decks, bisecting downtown, hardly turning, rearranging

Table 1. Indicators of Auto Dependence, Metropolitan Northwest, Early 1990s

Vancouver's compact form translates into higher transit ridership, a smaller vehicle fleet, and substantially less driving.

	Greater Portland	Greater Seattle	Greater Vancouver
Share of population in low-density neighborhoods	89%	91%	55%
Single-family houses as share of all residences	69%	68%	49%
Monthly transit trips per person	5	3	9
Motor vehicles per hundred people	85	79	60
Daily vehicle miles per person	24	24	15

Sources and definitions: see endnote 75. One kilometer = 0.62 mile.

the city according to the dictates of what traffic engineers call "high-speed geometrics." In Portland, the freeway veers wide of downtown, skirting its periphery and not exceeding eight lanes. In Vancouver, the continuation of I-5, Highway 99, turns from a limited-access expressway to an average-size arterial street when it crosses the city limits.

Was sprawl inevitable? As Henry Richmond, former head of 1,000 Friends of Oregon, and Saunders Hillyer of the National Growth Management Leadership Project in Washington, D.C., write, "Sprawl was not decreed by God, nor is it an immutable expression of the American character, love affair with the automobile, or dream of a house in the suburbs. To a great extent it has been shaped by public policies." Governments—not the invisible hand or the American Dream—gave the Northwest sprawl. And governments can give the Northwest something better.[76]

SOLUTIONS

THE TOWN

Vancouver's West End shows how the heart of a city can be, but it says nothing about what to do in a suburb. On the edges of greater Portland, the answer is emerging: Fill it in, mix it up, reconnect it. Turn it into a neighborhood. Not necessarily a high-rise neighborhood like the West End but something like an old-fashioned town—or an old-fashioned streetcar neighborhood. In the Northwest, this idea of filling in the urban universe with walkable, low-rise neighborhoods goes by several names, including "urban villages," "mixed use, medium density," "transit-oriented development," and "pedestrian pocket."

As exemplary as Portland's downtown is, its suburbs are hundreds of square miles of compartmentalized, low-density sprawl. And greater Portland is expecting a million newcomers in the next few decades. Its next challenge lies in Washington County, the frontier of sprawl west of town that is a farm district growing bumper crops of winter wheat, berries, fruits, nuts, and wine grapes. On this fertile soil, road builders want to pour concrete around the city to form a Western Bypass route. A group of grassroots opponents named Sensible Transportation Options for People (STOP) took issue with that plan and started to make a ruckus. Eventually, other groups were drawn to the cause, including the state's veteran land use planning advocate, 1,000 Friends of Oregon, or "Thousand Friends." The group decided to make Washington County a test case, so it brought in experts from across the country to cook up a less auto-bound alternative.[77]

The resulting plan goes by the acronym LUTRAQ, for Land Use, Transportation, and Air Quality. Under the LUTRAQ banner, the experts proposed a future for a hundred square miles of Washington County that would look like the old streetcar neighborhoods. They meticulously revised the transportation models that aid government planners in Oregon. These widely used computer-simulation models are good at projecting car traffic under conventional suburban land use planning because they assume that people do not walk anywhere, which might as well be true in such settings.

The experts used the revised models to compare the LUTRAQ option with the bypass-plus-conventional-land-use option. In the computer simulation, LUTRAQ reduced total driving, the share of driving that was done alone, traffic accidents, traffic congestion, the share of households with more than one automobile, and per capita consumption of gasoline. It also allowed twice as many children to walk and bike to school.[78]

Meeky Blizzard, one of the instigators of STOP, is touring the route of the proposed Western Bypass and talking, over the traffic noise, about LUTRAQ. She begins on the Sunset Highway, a corridor of industrial parks where Intel, Sequent, and other high-tech firms have been setting up shop. The county is pining for more and has laid miles of new road network across vacant farmland as an inducement for firms to move there. Almost everyone who works in this "Sunset Corridor," Meeky says, drives here from other counties. The wages in these plants are fairly low, and for decades Washington County sought to exclude affordable housing to prevent poor people from moving in.[79]

The LUTRAQ solution to the Sunset Corridor, Meeky says, is a simple, if radical, idea: "Put the housing and the jobs in the same place." Once, industrial zones needed to be kept far from housing because they were full of smelly factories that menaced public health. But today, many high-tech facilities pollute less per acre than a housing development. After six years of pressure from

STOP, Meeky proudly notes, "The radical thoughts are coming back to us from the folks who have the microphone." Affordable housing is now part of the plan for Washington County.

The next stop on the sprawl tour is the Tualatin Valley Highway, a major east-west route connecting Portland to fast-growing Forest Grove. It is run-of-the-mill commercial strip. "Imagine getting off a bus here," Meeky says. "There's poor lighting, two lanes in either direction, and a suicide lane in the middle. For bus stops, there are no shelters—just signs on telephone poles beside the ditch. And the traffic lights are easily a quarter mile apart. The fire and rescue people call this Big Gulp Gulch because people are routinely hit going across the street to the 7-Eleven. And despite how hard it is to take the bus here, this particular bus route has one of the highest riderships in the system." The residential areas nearby house many families who cannot afford second cars.

On the surface, Meeky says, LUTRAQ's plan for here is simple: "The pedestrian infrastructure is not complete—no sidewalks, no crosswalks, no bus shelters." This problem is widespread. Throughout the Northwest, sidewalks are too narrow; they should allow three people to walk abreast comfortably. In Seattle, fully one-third of streets lack sidewalks, and in many suburbs, sidewalks are absent.[80] **14** **Complete the pedestrian infrastructure.**

There is a bigger issue on Tualatin Valley Highway, too—what Meeky calls "building orientation." Regional planning rules in greater Portland say that new commercial buildings must be located the "minimum practical distance from the street," but on commercial roads like this one, most stores sit behind their parking. Big retailers such as Wal-Mart and Safeway customarily stand 500 feet from the curb, which makes walking to them a bit like crossing a firing range. LUTRAQ, Meeky says, would put all commercial buildings at the sidewalk. According to research by Thousand Friends, putting all commercial buildings at the street, with parking facilities tucked underneath or behind, reduces driving per person in a neighborhood by 15 percent.[81]

The next stop is zoned residential, a housing tract called the Highlands. "Take a look at this," Meeky says, shaking her head and pulling off the highway. It is a street of brand-new houses, or more precisely, of brand-new garages. From her vantage point, she can see the driveways spreading out from the street and the double garage doors lining up toward the horizon. "Can you see any front doors or porches?" None are visible. "For all you know, cars live here. 'Snout houses' is what a friend of mine calls them. The only way to figure out which one is yours is to go down the street pressing your garage door opener." Front porches, according to Meeky, are built on the assumption that people will be arriving on foot. They are superfluous here because no one could possibly arrive on foot. You can hardly even leave this subdivision without an automobile. **15** **Build front porches.**

The LUTRAQ answer to the Highlands is in evidence at a place called Tualatin Commons, a pedestrian pocket in the city of Tualatin. It is a tight cluster of town houses, flats, and single-family homes—some of them with porches. They face inward on a shared open space as buildings do in some New England villages. Paths crisscross the community and parking is concentrated at the rear. A community center is planned, along with office spaces and foot paths to stores and transit stops. LUTRAQ calls for communities like this one at every light-rail station.

Meeky talks about gradually changing what is already built, too. Four decades of subdivisions need to be filled in, she says, first with granny flats, and later with smaller lots, town houses, and multifamily units mixed among the single-family ones. **16** **Fill in suburban neighborhoods.** They also need to be mixed-up, with pockets of stores and workplaces inserted into them. And finally, they need to be connected up: the maze of suburban cul-de-sacs needs to be turned into a functional grid. How is unclear, but maybe narrow, single-lane roads, pedestrian routes, transit-only streets, and other low-traffic rights-of-way would do the trick.

Resistance to these ideas is strong, but Meeky believes people will jump at the opportunity for change if they are confident it will be for the better. She proposes a participatory approach that works slowly and meticulously, block by block, fixing easy problems first and building trust all around. She cites Portland public works commissioner Earl Blumenaur, for example, for his "neighbor walks." He hijacks a few city staff members, invites a photographer, and meets local residents for a Saturday walk around the neighborhood. Together they look at problem street corners, vacant lots, school zones, and traffic patterns, and they plan improvements. She points to the Hillsboro Vision group, a citizen committee that has helped the neighborhood of Hillsboro create a shared vision of what their neighborhood should look like after the inevitable development comes—and has gone on to embed that vision in the city's comprehensive plan. **17 Hold a community meeting to develop a shared vision of the future.**

Vision is crucial, Meeky insists. It is also unifying. People from the city and the suburbs all want the same things: safe, convenient neighborhoods with a sense of community. "What we're talking about isn't from outer space; it's something old and well liked. It's the kind of thing that people fly to Europe to see."

Terry Moore agrees. A member of greater Portland's governing Metropolitan council, she led public workshops with hundreds of business leaders, elected officials, and citizens during 1994. At each one, she asked participants to list the things their communities should have in fifty years. "When people put down everything they want, they get a city that's many times more dense than we could ever imagine" based on projected population growth. "They want to have a movie theater. They want to have their shops, and restaurants, and Starbucks. And they want to be able to walk. And they want to have a community center. And they want to have apartments. And they want to have jobs" in their communities. Above all, they want safe places for children to play.[82]

On the other end of metropolitan Portland, the city of Gresham is putting the pieces together. Mayor Gussie McRobert, arriving at the Gresham rail station in a downpour, laments the hundreds of feet of parking lots that separate the station from the nearest building. When the MAX was built in the 1980s, she explains, Gresham was so resistant that it put the rail line wide of the business core. "That was before I had any say-so around here," she says with a smile. "Now the downtown businesses are kicking themselves. We're going to put town hall in that parking lot right next to the station, and we're planning a 200-acre mixed-use development nearby." The market for mixed-use, medium-density real estate close to MAX is red-hot, she says. "The only problem is the banks won't finance higher density. I swear they are hidebound by tradition."[83]

In the early 1990s, Gussie launched something called Gresham Vision, a community-wide effort to define what kind of place Gresham ought to be. The conclusion was compact development surrounded by open space—especially on the lava buttes that ring town. So Gussie put an open space rescue levy on the ballot and used the $10 million proceeds to buy up property on the buttes by the hundreds of acres. In town, she helped reduce the average size of housing lots; "people don't want big yards anymore," she insists. And she has pushed for well-designed higher density and mixing of uses everywhere else she can. "If you don't do these things," she explains, "you end up with nothing but asphalt."

The downtown business people "got the fever" of pedestrian-friendly development. Now there are benches, trees, wider sidewalks, and traffic-calming "bubbles" in the center of town. Combining density with open space is working well. Gresham is booming, and the share of residents who work in town rather than commuting has increased to half over the past decade. Downtown business people have even begun coming to town meetings demanding greater density and reduced parking. For the future, Gussie wants more of the same, plus something more: "I want to put housing right in the middle of our office parks."

SOLUTIONS

PRICES

The tollgate raises its mechanical arm to let out another car, this one a steely gray sedan trailing bluish smoke. The auto pulls away from the darkened booth, glides up a ramp, and disappears into daylight. Leaning against a wall in the exhaust-filled garage, Todd Litman is watching the gate rise and fall. In the building above are the Victoria offices of the B.C. Ministry of Transportation and Highways. This is the underground parking for the province's high priests of motorized velocity, and a good place to ponder the cost and price of the automobile. The gap between the two is a principal cause of the tensions between the car and the city. Closing that gap is both a critical counterpart to effective land use planning and a powerful tool to promote compact land use.[84]

Todd, an economist and principal of the Victoria Transport Policy Institute, spends a lot of time thinking about closing the gap. "The financial price Northwest motorists pay for each mile they drive is 37¢, but the full cost is $1.05" (see Table 2.) By Todd's reckoning, motorists make nonmonetary payments—in time and in assuming the risk of accidents—worth another 34¢ per mile. "So motorists pick up two-thirds of the cost of driving." They bill other people, especially nondrivers, the poor, and taxpayers, for the remaining third. In economic terminology, these costs imposed on others are "external." At first, 34¢ in external costs does not sound like much; it's not even bus fare. But consider that vehicles in the Northwest travel about 100 billion miles a year.[85]

What offenses are counted in this 34¢ a mile? Todd ticks off the costs as the tollgate rises to discharge a sputtering Mercedes. The biggest costs—he tallies them at a nickel or more each—are air pollution, sprawl, congestion, accident risk imposed on others, and subsidies for parking. The smaller costs are worth pennies or fractions of pennies apiece. They include waste generation, water and noise pollution, land values lost to roads and parking facilities, and a litany of auto-related government expenses not fully recovered from fuel and vehicle taxes—such as road construction and maintenance, military protection of oil fields and supply lines, traffic policing, and emergency services at auto accidents.[86]

To calculate these figures, Todd has synthesized the findings of thousands of scholars and had his analysis scrutinized by scores of

Table 2. Estimated Full Cost of Driving a Mile in the United States, Early 1990s

Drivers bill one-third of the cost of driving to others.

	Paid by Driver		Not Paid by Driver
Monetary Costs	**Fixed Driver Costs:** Vehicle purchase Vehicle maintenance Insurance and registration Home parking	24¢	Subsidized roadwork and emergency services "Free" parking Defense of oil supplies Productivity lost to congestion
	Variable Driver Costs: Fuel and fuel taxes Tires and oil "Pay" parking	13¢	
	Total Monetary:	37¢	10¢
Non-monetary Costs	Personal time Stress Own risk of accident		Others' time lost to congestion Environmental damage Risk of accident to others
	Total Nonmonetary:	34¢	24¢
Total Cost:		71¢	34¢

Note: Assigning monetary values to nonmonetary costs is problematic. These figures reflect the best estimates published in the economic literature, as synthesized by Todd Litman of the Victoria Transport Policy Institute.

Sources: see endnote 85.

economists and transportation experts. To estimate the costs of driving's negative effects on bodies of water, for example, he reviewed the scientific literature on the damages to aquatic systems caused by the automotive industry, automotive infrastructure, and vehicle fleet. He studied the impacts of spills from oil tankers and pipelines, fluids dripping from crankcases, used oil poured into storm drains, road salt and herbicides disturbing streams, leaking underground fuel storage tanks, air pollutants that settle into bodies of water, and parking-lot runoff laced with toxic metals and hydrocarbons. He reviewed the effects of pavement on the hydrological cycle: pavement concentrates storm water, reduces surface permeability and groundwater recharge, and increases flooding and drying of streams. The construction of roads, road cuts, and culverts truncates natural stream and shoreline processes, such as sediment movement, fish passage, temperature gradients, and nutrient cycling.[87]

After dissecting existing cost estimates on each of these types of damages, Todd estimated the costs of the effects on bodies of water at 1.3¢ per vehicle-mile. This figure may be a bit too low or too high, Todd suggests as a minivan passes. "Either way, it's closer to the truth than zero—which is what that driver is paying."

Underpricing automobile use leads to massive transfers of wealth—and well-being—from people who drive less to people who drive more. Households with annual incomes less than $10,000 drive a fourth as much on average as households with incomes more than $40,000. And urban households drive about a third as much as suburban households. Furthermore, approximately one-tenth of northwesterners belong to households that own no automobile; these people pay all the external costs of driving. Car-less households are disproportionately made up of the disabled, elderly, female, and poor.[88]

Table 3. Selected Measures of Vehicle Use and Costs, Pacific Northwest, 1994

British Columbians drive less than their neighbors, partly because of higher costs of owning and operating a vehicle.

	Gasoline Consumption per Capita (gallons)	Vehicle Travel per Capita (miles)	Net Fuel Tax (US¢/gallon)	Average Insurance Premium (US$/year)
British Columbia	294	~6,000	59¢	~$700
Washington	462	8,880	32¢	$588
Oregon	457	9,540	42¢	$535
Idaho	466	10,230	33¢	$402

Note: In B.C., fuel consumption was 1,100 liters, and estimated vehicle travel 9,700 kilometers, per capita; net fuel taxes were 21Can¢, and estimated insurance premiums Can$960.

Sources and defininitions: see endnote 89.

Underpricing automobile use also leads to massive overuse of driving. Compare British Columbia, where prices come closer to full costs, with Idaho, Oregon, and Washington (see Table 3.) British Columbians drive substantially less, but full pricing of external costs would reduce vehicle travel even more. It could lower driving rates by half over a decade because, all things considered, as much as half of current driving actually does more harm than good. Furthermore, people drive more than they need to relative to the current price—even in B.C.—because of the disproportionate share of expenses that are fixed, rather than variable.[89]

"Owning a car is very expensive," says Todd, "but driving a car is very cheap. The purchase price of the car, insurance, registration, residential parking—all those you're going to pay whether you drive one mile or 20,000 miles a year." Together, these fixed costs average $2,500 a year or more in the United States. When making daily decisions about where to go and how to get there, car owners consider only the variable costs of driving: fuel, parking (where it is charged), and a portion of vehicle maintenance, new oil, and tires. These costs average 13¢ a mile in the United States. The largest and most visible cost is fuel, at about a nickel a mile, and its inflation-adjusted price on the streets of the Northwest is lower today than ever before.[90]

The total cost of driving, then, is about a dollar a mile. The price is roughly a dime.

Converting fixed costs into variable costs would give people an incentive to drive less without increasing average expenses per driver. Insurance and parking are the costs most ripe for conversion. **18 Sell insurance by the slice.**

Drivers pay an average of 7¢ a mile for auto insurance—more than they pay for fuel. The more you drive, the higher the probability you will get in an accident. Yet auto insurers put almost no weight on mileage in calculating insurance rates. The California Insurance Department reported in December 1994 that major insurers in that state underweighted mileage in their risk formulas by factors ranging from two to twenty-two. They overweighted place of residence in their calculations, with the result that car owners in poor, minority neighborhoods in big cities paid premiums two to three times higher than similar car owners living in affluent suburbs.[91]

Because insurance is not sold by the mile, says Todd Litman, "Nobody is going to say, I'm not going to take this trip by car to save insurance." This pattern of auto insurance is socially inequitable, economically inefficient, and environmentally destructive. There are several viable ways to sell insurance by the slice, the simplest being simply to require insurers to account accurately for mileage in their rates.

A more comprehensive and efficient solution, however, is to convert to no-fault, pay-at-the-pump insurance. Motorists would buy insurance through a flat surcharge of perhaps 40¢ on each gallon of gasoline—a charge rolled into the listed gas price just like gas taxes. State government would randomly divide all registered vehicles into blocks of several thousand each, and insurers would bid to cover each block of vehicles. The state would automatically forward the insurance payments collected by gas stations to insurers in proportion to how many blocks they insured. Because the system would replace the current litigious system with a no-fault regime that paid legitimate costs and losses—but not the legal fees and sales costs that consume roughly half of every insurance dollar today—motorists would actually pay less for insurance. Best of all, because everybody would buy insurance at the pump, there would no longer be uninsured motorists.[92]

Insurance-by-the-gallon would make insurance costs a factor in people's daily transportation and destination planning, even while reducing the total cost of driving.

Converting parking to a variable cost is a similar opportunity. **19 Deregulate parking.** Todd says, "Americans end 99 percent of auto trips at free parking spaces. No, not free," he corrects himself. "Somebody pays for them." The parking spaces in the B.C. Ministry's garage are among the tiny fraction where drivers pay for exactly what they use.

Parking is the dominant land use in urban areas. A typical commercial development dedicates more land to parking than to the buildings that the parking serves. The Northwest has two-and-a-half times as many parking spaces as motor vehicles. At an average rental value per space of $30 a month, parking a car is worth about twice as much as the fuel the car burns. It comes to

10¢ a mile: a penny a mile for meters, lots, and garages, 4¢ a mile in fixed costs—mostly rent or mortgage for parking at home—and a nickel a mile chipped in by taxpayers and businesses.[93]

Drivers do not pay per use for parking because antiquated provisions in zoning and tax codes, along with misguided street designs, have artificially increased the supply of parking—glutting the market and causing the price to drop toward zero. Fixing these flaws would force the pricing of some parking immediately and of most parking eventually.

Zoning codes enforce a tremendous oversupply of parking. In the sixteen most populous counties and cities in the Northwest, off-street parking requirements are omnipresent. Rural and suburban jurisdictions require even more parking than cities. For houses, the requirement is usually two spaces per house. Office buildings are required to provide up to four spaces per 1,000 square feet of floor space. And in much of the region, retail developers are required to devote more space to cars than they do to people. In Pierce County, Washington; in Washington County, Oregon; and in Sonoma County, California, for example, the law mandates five parking spaces per 1,000 square feet of floorspace; in a normal lot, that works out to 1,500 square feet of pavement.[94]

The rationale for requiring off-street parking is that it eliminates problems such as shoppers filling the curbside spaces in nearby neighborhoods. But obligatory off-street parking actually costs people much more than stricter parking enforcement would. "Because businesses and households are forced to spend so much money providing parking, we pay more for the tomatoes at the grocery store, get lower wages, and pay extra for housing," says Todd as he walks up the ramp. He continues talking as he strolls through central Victoria, a district that—along with Vancouver's West End and downtown Portland—is among the best places in the Northwest to be a pedestrian.

To make parking a variable cost, the Northwest could strike all off-street parking requirements from zoning codes. Deregulation would allow the market to decide how much parking space to provide and how to pay for it. Many new developments would include much less parking, lowering costs, especially for the poor. Including parking facilities in new multifamily buildings increases construction costs by up to 18 percent. Portland recently permitted the construction of a downtown low-income housing project without any off-street parking, a waiver that likely shaved more than $10,000 off the cost of each apartment.[95]

The change would affect existing developments as well. The owners of buildings surrounded by seas of concrete would have new choices. They could expand, sell off land to others, or turn parking into landscaped plazas. Even homeowners would have new options, such as converting parking space to living or gardening space. It might take ten years for the oversupply of parking space to be absorbed by these changes, but scarcity—and a market—would inevitably develop. Employers and retailers would start charging for parking, so nondriving workers and shoppers would no longer subsidize their peers who drive. Prices, in short, would tell the truth.

Where communities are still being laid out, streets can be made narrower—a proposal the cities of Olympia and Missoula are both considering. Todd estimates that only about one-third of the average-width current street is needed for basic access by foot, ambulance, and transit vehicles and for utility lines. The remainder exists to serve private cars, mostly for parking. Metering or otherwise charging for curbside parking where possible would at least ensure that drivers pay rent for their use of public rights-of-way. Parking revenues that a neighborhood generates could then be deposited in a fund for community improvements. **❷⓪ Use parking meter proceeds for neighborhood funds.** Otherwise, the

political opposition might be overwhelming. Seattle Mayor Norm
Rice, otherwise wildly popular, was nearly thrown out of office
for raising the price of parking at downtown meters during his
first term. He doubled the rate from a dollar an hour. Habitu-
ated motorists howled, although they kept right on parking at
the meters. In the end, Rice not only rolled back the parking
rate but also committed public funds to expand downtown parking for shoppers.[96]

In the long term, cities could convert some of the space now
devoted to on-street parking to uses such as broader sidewalks,
street trees, and bicycle or transit lanes. They could even auction
off excess street space to property owners. The reallocation of
street space could have profound impacts. In relatively flat Victoria,
at any given time there are as many people riding bicycles as buses,
even though bicyclists must mix with dangerous traffic. Bicycle
use would soar if cyclists were given shielded lanes away from cars.
Minor bicycle facility improvements in hilly Seattle increased bike
commuting to downtown by 28 percent from 1992 to 1995.[97]

Similarly, pedestrian travel could increase with wider sidewalks and better crosswalks. Todd pauses on Douglas Street, a
busy thoroughfare in the heart of town. "Right here, at midday on
a weekday, pedestrians outnumber motorists, but motorists get five
times as much street space. Car traffic is flowing smoothly; pedestrian traffic is terribly congested."

Another egregious flaw in revenue codes is the failure to treat
free parking for employees as a form of income—as a taxable
benefit. Free employee parking is currently ubiquitous: in King
County, Washington, which includes Seattle and is the Northwest's
most populous local jurisdiction, more than 70 percent of workers park for free.[98]

Under B.C. and Canadian law, free parking is taxable income,
but Revenue Canada makes only token efforts to enforce the rule.

Park or Ride?

Washington's Commute Trip Reduction Law requires large employers to designate a staff member as employee transportation coordinator and to establish plans to reduce the share of workers who arrive alone in their cars. Boeing, which has had an employee transportation program since 1942, relies heavily on vanpools and public transit. Microsoft workers favor carpools and coordinate rides on-line from their desks. And Nordstrom's most successful program has been its guarantee of a ride home to any worker who commutes without a car and has a family emergency while at work.

Key Bank, meanwhile, has successfully tested reducing commute lengths rather than vehicle numbers. Because fewer than a fifth of Key Bank employees work at the branch closest to their home, the company figured it could do more good matching job openings and home sites. At thirty branches enrolled in the program, the average commute length declined by 17 percent over the first year of the program. Overall, Washington's Commute Trip Reduction Law took 120,000 cars off the road every weekday in its first two years of operation.

Unfortunately, car traffic is notorious for expanding to fill road and parking space available, so these voluntary measures may have been offset by new trips taken by others. If parking were priced, however, trip reduction efforts would become an automatic part of everyone's lives.

Parking pressures—not trip reduction mandates—were the motive force behind three other successful efforts. At the University of Washington in Seattle and Boise State University, parking prices rose at the same time that all students were given free transit passes. Saint Luke's Hospital in Boise, under community pressure to reduce spillover parking on neighborhood streets, instituted one of the region's most comprehensive trip reduction programs. Saint Luke's provides preferential parking for carpools, flexible start-of-work times for nondrivers, free taxi rides in family emergencies, and free bus and vanpool passes. Dedicated to health promotion, the hospital also installed showers, lockers, and bicycle racks, and gives away bike locks and walking shoes.[99]

Indeed, even offices of government agencies in greater Vancouver give away parking worth Can$26 million a year. In the United States, under the Internal Revenue Code, employers may provide parking worth up to $155 a month to employees as an untaxed fringe benefit—equivalent to pretax income that exceeds $2,000 a year. They may also provide transit fares, but only up to $60 a month, and they may not provide anything toward bicycling or walking expenses. Among Northwest states with income taxes, only California even has a policy on employee parking. It specifies that employee parking is only free of state income tax if employees have the option of cashing-out the benefit: they must have the choice of getting to work without their cars and receiving the dollar value of the free parking in cash. Tests of "cashing-out parking" in Los Angeles show that as many as two in five commuters take the money and leave their wheels at home. These results are encouraging because commuting accounts for a fourth of all auto trips.[100] **㉑ Ask your employer to take back your parking space and give you a $2,000 raise.**

If the Northwest reformed insurance and parking in these ways, the price of driving would more than double, but total driving expense would decline. Driving would decrease by perhaps a third over the long term if these big, fixed, annual costs were chopped up into small, regular, variable costs.[101]

A property tax is actually two conflicting taxes rolled into one. It is a tax on the value of buildings and a tax on the value of the land under those buildings. As experience in Australia, New Zealand, Taiwan, and Pennsylvania shows, shifting the tax from the former to the latter aids compact development while suppressing land speculation, promoting productive investment, and tempering housing costs, especially for the poor. It does these things because of the unique nature of land values.[102]

In land values, location counts for everything. Land in a crime-infested, rundown neighborhood is worth a fraction as much as an identical lot in a safe, popular neighborhood. Paradoxically, property owners can increase their building values by improving their buildings, but they can do nothing to change their land values. Only their neighbors, government, and society can do that. Government actions are especially important, and they usually increase land values. If a city builds a park, a province expands transportation infrastructure, or a nation restores a historic landmark near a parcel, the land's value will rise. Curiously, property-rights defenders decry reductions in land values caused by government, which they call "takings," and demand compensation for it. But they do not call for landowners to repay public coffers for the more common "givings"—where government actions increase land values.[103]

Location matters a great deal to people. In King County, for example, the assessed value of real property exceeded $100 billion in 1993: $61 billion of it was the value of private buildings, approximately what it would cost to reconstruct these structures. The remaining $46 billion was the value of land—what people were willing to pay purely for location.[104]

And location matters more to people as time goes by. As incomes rise, people spend an increasing share of their earnings on location. Historically, urban land values have increased faster than population, the consumer price index, or income. A typical property buyer in King County in the 1950s paid about one-tenth of the purchase price for land and nine-tenths for the building; in 1993, land accounted for 43 percent of the purchase price. In economic terms, rising wealth is capitalized in land values; in common parlance, to quote comedian Will Rogers, "Buy land, because they ain't makin' any more of it."[105]

These peculiarities of land values make land speculation possible. Most successful investments—whether in businesses or buildings—create salable products not otherwise available. The investor makes money, and consumers have more of what they want. But successful land speculation—the purchase of land for the purpose of holding it until its value increases—fails the public. It does not create any salable good or service; it prevents full use of premium sites. The investor makes money, and society has less of what its members want. Land speculation explains why roughly 5 percent of private urban land in Pacific Northwest cities is vacant, while perhaps three times as much is underused.[106]

Land speculation is parasitic, not productive. Its antidote is to shift the property tax off buildings and onto land. **22 Exempt buildings from property tax.** Where such exemptions have been granted—in dozens of North American jurisdictions such as Pittsburgh and thousands of localities in Australia and New Zealand—it has resulted in aggressive development of the most valuable sites, almost all of which were in cities rather than suburbs. Density increases. The apartment and office space supplies increase. Rents fall. Parking supply declines as parking lots—a standard holding pattern for land speculators—are developed. Finally, shifting the property tax onto land is highly progressive, because landownership is extremely concentrated in the hands of the rich. Those who own no land benefit enormously, and even middle-class homeowners benefit, because their houses are usually worth more than their land.[107]

Improving the accuracy of assessments is equally critical because many jurisdictions currently undervalue land, effectively subsidizing speculation. The accuracy of property value assessments in the state of Washington is as low as 70 percent of full market value in some counties, and the statewide average for 1995 was below 90 percent—a gap that meant hundreds of millions of dollars of windfalls for landowners. British Columbian assessments, in contrast, reflected more than 95 percent of market prices in 1994.[108]

Vancouver's above-average density is partly a consequence of the province's state-of-the-art assessment techniques—techniques so much better than the norm that the B.C. Assessment Authority sells its computerized data management system to other jurisdictions. It helps that the province hires assessors through a competitive personnel process, whereas most Northwest jurisdictions elect theirs. Assessment is a professional skill: there is always a right answer. Leadership qualities and political philosophy—matters best judged by voters—are irrelevant. In Oregon, where counties decide how to select assessors but most are elected, several counties are considering switching over to an appointment system.[109]

Taxes and government spending in the Northwest penalize work, savings, and enterprise, while subsidizing sprawl, driving, and other unsustainable activities. Reversing these practices will help both the economy and the environment. **23 Shift taxes off work and onto pollution.** It will also raise the price of driving closer to its true cost. The Northwest can do that by decreasing sales, payroll, and income taxes while phasing in a set of taxes on vehicle use and vehicle fuels.[110]

The most important of these taxes would be national, state, or provincial carbon taxes—levies on all fossil fuels in proportion to the greenhouse gases released through their combustion. The tax would be best applied as far up the production line as possible. Fossil fuels extracted in North America would be taxed at the wellhead or mouth of the coal mine, and imported fuels would be taxed at the port of entry. Upstream taxation minimizes administrative burdens and ensures that the proper price incentive travels throughout the economy—to refiners, processors, transporters, and retailers, as well as to final consumers.[111]

Autos' other external costs, from local air and water pollution to accident risk to congestion, could be transferred to drivers in different ways. Possible mechanisms are numerous—from simply raising fuel taxes to instituting by-the-mile charges that vary with vehicle weight, emissions rates, and road congestion at time of use. Ideally, drivers would pay by the mile, the minute, or the gram of pollution for use of roads, parking spaces, and shared air and water resources, much as consumers currently pay for long-distance telephone calls. The information revolution makes such proposals, which have long been advanced by economists, technically possible.[112]

California is experimenting with high-tech toll roads, where cars are charged for road use like so many groceries sweeping across checkout scanners. The Oregon Environmental Council in Portland, in conjunction with the three-county governing council Metro, is leading a metropolitan dialogue on roadway pricing. And planners in Seattle and Vancouver have studied the subject; the former rejected the proposal because it struck conservatives as a new tax, and Vancouver postponed action for fear of raising motorists' hackles.[113]

The nut of the problem is to tie these new fees to reductions in other taxes—especially viciously regressive ones such as flat taxes on sales and payrolls—and to use the revenue for the general support of government, not simply for transportation-related expenses. All Northwest jurisdictions except British Columbia dedicate gas tax revenues for roadwork; in Washington, that provision is written into the state constitution. This practice creates a revolving door of more driving and more road building.[114]

Mobility is a means; it deserves no subsidy. Taxpayers have bankrolled the car and sprawl for decades, with money for transit thrown in as a palliative; the only thing worth subsidizing now is the city. Perhaps states should dedicate all fuel-tax revenues to schools, parks, and especially police—since crime is the leading motivator of urban flight—leaving highway departments to propose tax levies each time they think they need a new road.

THE UPSHOT

CHOICES

Pricing auto travel better—by reforming insurance, parking, and taxes—would nourish current and as yet unimagined alternatives. It would spur development of cleaner, safer cars and cleaner, safer auto infrastructure. British Columbia has already become the first Canadian province to adopt the tough Californian standards for low-emission vehicles and clean-burning gasoline. And the possibilities are encouraging.

Energy analyst Amory Lovins of the Rocky Mountain Institute argues that private cars could be made to travel 300 miles per gallon with vast improvements in safety and performance by combining the best new composite materials with a revolutionary "hybrid electric" drive train. A team at Western Washington University in Bellingham has applied some of these design techniques to create a prototype that gets 200 miles per gallon.[115]

Full-cost pricing might lead to thriving car cooperatives, like the incipient one in Eugene, Oregon, or the thousands that are found in Germany. In a co-op, you pay for your driving only by the mile and the minute, and thus can save your money when you don't need to drive. Full-cost pricing would also lead to improvements in transit service, pedestrian and carpooling facilities, and every other means of mobility. It would make people clean the spider webs off their bicycles: an estimated 1 million bikes are sitting in the garages and basements of greater Seattle.[116]

Over time, people would reorganize where they do what. They would choose residences closer to work, friends, and shopping. Employers would locate closer to suppliers, residences, and services. Neighborhood stores and front porches would develop again.

Through the effect of millions of voluntary choices, sprawl would reverse itself. Cities' footprints would contract. The estimated one-fourth of urban land that is devoted to the automobile and the somewhat smaller portion that is held in speculation would begin to fill up with new buildings, increasing density and reducing auto dependence. Cars would be one choice among many, and they would continue to be used on trips where, in the drivers' judgments, the benefits were worth the price. In a market economy, that is as it should be.

Is enough happening in Northwest cities? No. Vancouver's population is growing by a West End's worth each year, and much of that growth is taking place in snout houses outside the city. Close to two-thirds of workers in the metropolis now commute from one suburb to another, rendering the core less relevant. In Portland, sprawling residential development continues despite the urban growth boundary and the comprehensive plans. And greater Seattle, despite a statewide growth management act and a well-regarded comprehensive land use plan, has still sanctioned the development of 400 square miles of rural land by 2020. Indeed, many of the ten county land use plans developed under the state Growth Management Act consist simply of planned sprawl. Collectively, they promise an average population density in twenty years lower than today's. In places like Boise, western Montana, the Canadian Okanagan valley, and the sunny side of Vancouver Island, sprawl is rampant, and population is growing at record rates.[117]

The Pacific Northwest has changed its vision and begun to change its policies, but it will take a while to see the results on the ground. Yet step by step, change is happening. **24 Give this book to the person beside you on the bus.**

Northwesterners transformed the urban landscape in the half-century since World War II. And the transformation has not slowed. In the next half-century, they will undoubtedly rebuild much of what now exists. The question is what they will build. If they choose wisely, they will create cities with vital economies, safe and secure neighborhoods, diminishing impacts on the global environment, and flourishing communities. They will create cities where—with almost no one noticing at first—the number of automobiles declines. Not because cars are less useful but because they are less necessary. If Northwesterners choose well, they will end up with a human habitat worthy of its creators. And they will set an example for the world.

NOTES

1. John C. Ryan, *State of the Northwest* (Seattle: Northwest Environment Watch [NEW], 1994; Alan Thein Durning, *This Place on Earth* (Seattle: Sasquatch Books, in press).
2. Chapter based on Gordon Price, private communication, Nov. 19, 1994, and Gordon Price, "Tale of Three Cities," *New Pacific (Vancouver)*, autumn 1992.
3. "Motor vehicles" refers to all motorized on-road vehicles except motor-cycles. Causes of death from J. Michael McGinnis and William H. Foege, "Actual Causes of Death in the United States," *Journal of the American Medical Association*, Nov. 10, 1993, and private communications with state offices of vital statistics. Deaths and injuries from Federal Highway Administration (FHWA), *Highway Statistics 1993* (D.C.: 1994), and Ministry of Transportation and Highways, Motor Vehicle Branch, *1993 Traffic Accident Statistics* (Ottawa: 1994). Relationship to fuel price, effects on young and old from National Safety Council, *Accident Facts, 1995* (Itasca, IL: 1995).
4. Environment 2010, *1991 State of the Environment* (Olympia: Wash. State Dept. of Ecology, 1992); City of Vancouver Task Force on Atmospheric Change, "Clouds of Change," Vancouver, Jun. 1990.
5. Weight from Christopher Flavin and Alan Durning, *Building on Success* (D.C.: Worldwatch Institute, 1988). Automotive share from John C. Ryan, "Greenhouse Gases on the Rise," *NEW Indicator*, Aug. 1995.
6. Steve Nadis and James J. MacKenzie, *Car Trouble* (Boston: Beacon Press, 1993). Crop value from B.C. Round Table on the Economy and the Environment (B.C. Round Table), *Georgia Basin Initiative* (Victoria: 1993). John C. Ryan, "Roads Take Toll on Salmon, Grizzlies, Taxpayers," *NEW Indicator*, Dec. 1995.
7. Alan Thein Durning, "Vehicles Outnumber Drivers in Pacific Northwest," *NEW Indicator*, Jan. 1995.
8. Vehicle-miles from FHWA, *Highway Statistics* (D.C.: various editions), and Office of Highway Information Management, FHWA, D.C., unpublished data. Share of trips in cars estimated from Ray M. Northam, "Transportation," in Philip L. Jackson and A. Jon Kimerling, eds., *Atlas of the Pacific Northwest* (Corvallis: Ore. State Univ. Press, 1993); from B.C. Round Table, *State of Sustainability* (Victoria: Crown Publications, 1994); and B.C. Energy Council, *Planning Today for Tomorrow's Energy* (Vancouver: 1994). Figure 1 U.S. Bureau of the Census, *Urbanized Areas of the United*

States and Puerto Rico (D.C.: 1993), and U.S. Bureau of the Census, *Census of Population: 1950, 1960,* and *1980,* Vol. 1, "Characteristics of the Population, Parts for Oregon, Washington and Idaho" (D.C.: 1952, 1963, and 1982). "Cities" refers to the "central places" in the Census Bureau's "urbanized areas." "Suburbs" refers to the Bureau's "urban fringe." "Towns" refers to all "urban areas" outside "urbanized areas." "Rural" is used as defined by the Bureau. Housing for Washington from Rhys Roth, *Redevelopment for Livable Communities* (Olympia: Wash. State Energy Office [WSEO], 1995).

9. Peter W. G. Newman and Jeffrey R. Kenworthy, *Cities and Automobile Dependence* (Brookfield, Vt.: Gower Technical, 1989). Cars per driver from American Automobile Manufacturers Association, *Facts and Figures '93* (Detroit: 1993). Trips per household from Doug Kelbaugh, (professor, Univ. of Wash. [U.W.], Seattle) presentation at conference, "Building with Values '93," Seattle, Nov. 12, 1993. Suburban-urban driving from John Holtzclaw, "Using Residential Patterns and Transit to Decrease Auto Dependence and Costs," Natural Resources Defense Council (NRDC), San Francisco, 1994.

10. Rhys Roth, *Municipal Strategies to Increase Pedestrian Travel* (Olympia: WSEO, 1994).

11. See U.S. Advisory Board on Child Abuse and Neglect, *Neighbors Helping Neighbors* (D.C.: U.S. Dept. of Health and Human Services, 1993); Carnegie Council on Adolescent Development, *Great Transitions* (N.Y.: Carnegie Corporation, 1995); and John Darrah, "Youths and Violence," *Seattle Post-Intelligencer*, Feb. 13, 1994.

12. Newman and Kenworthy, op. cit. note 9.

13. City of Vancouver, op. cit. note 4.

14. Newman and Kenworthy, op. cit. note 9. Figure 2: Greater Portland (1990) includes Clackamas, Multnomah, and Washington Counties; Greater Seattle (1994) includes King, Pierce, Kitsap, and Snohomish Counties; Greater Vancouver (1991) is the Vancouver Census Metropolitan Area, including the Greater Vancouver Regional District (GVRD), Pitt Meadows, and Maple Ridge. Shares of population determined by calculating population density at the census tract level, sorting by density, and reaggregating. Density thresholds from Newman and Kenworthy, op. cit. note 9. Seattle from Puget Sound Regional Council (PSRC), *Population and Housing Estimates, 1993 & 1994* (Seattle: 1995). Vancouver from Statistics Canada, *Profile of Census Tracts in Matsqui and Vancouver, Part A* (Ottawa: 1992). Portland from U.S. Bureau of the Census, *1990 Census of Population and Housing,* Census Bureau Data on CD-ROM (D.C.: 1992).

15. Newman and Kenworthy, op. cit. note 9.

16. Newman and Kenworthy, op. cit. note 9. Road space in B.C. cities from B.C. Round Table, op. cit. note 8. Other cities estimated from Tom Schueler,

"The Importance of Imperviousness," *Watershed Protection Techniques* (Silver Spring, Md: Center for Watershed Protection), fall 1994, and Sustainable Seattle, *Indicators of Sustainable Community 1995* (Seattle: MetroCenter Y.M.C.A., 1995).

17. Northwest densities from sources in note 14. Paragraph from Newman and Kenworthy, op. cit. note 9, except car ownership from Keith Bartholomew, "Making the Land Use, Transportation, Air Quality Connection," *PAS Memo* (American Planning Association), May 1993; pollution from Roth, op. cit. note 10.

18. Bus frequency and self-sufficiency from Preston Schiller and Jeffrey R. Kenworthy, "Prospects for Sustainable Transportation in the Pacific Northwest" (draft from Dr. Schiller in Kirkland, Wash.), Feb. 1996.

19. Newman and Kenworthy, op. cit. note 9; Holtzclaw, op. cit. note 9.

20. Price, "Tale of Three Cities," op. cit., note 2; Graeme Wynn and Timothy Oke, eds., *Vancouver and Its Region* (Vancouver: UBC Press, 1992).

21. Seattle Commons, Seattle, fact sheets, Feb. 1996.

22. Schiller and Kenworthy, op. cit. note 18.

23. Decision Data, "Puget Sound Housing Preference Study," Kirkland, Wash., 1994.

24. Neighborhoods just below medium density from sources in note 14.

25. David B. Goldstein, "Making Housing More Affordable: Correcting Misplaced Incentives in the Lending System," NRDC, San Francisco, Aug. 12 1994. Holtzclaw, op. cit. note 9.

26. Newman and Kenworthy, op. cit. note 9, Kelbaugh, op. cit. note 9.

27. GVRD, *Creating Our Future* (Vancouver: 1993); PSRC, *Vision 2020 Update* (Seattle: 1994); Metro, *Region 2040* (Portland: 1994).

28. PSRC, "Evaluating the Relationships between Advanced Telecommunications and Travel in the Central Puget Sound Region," Seattle, 1995.

29. Definition from Bartholomew, op. cit. note 17, and James Howard Kunstler, *The Geography of Nowhere* (N.Y.: Simon & Schuster, 1993).

30. Costs from Todd Litman, *Transportation Cost Analysis* (Victoria: Victoria Transport Policy Institute [VTPI], 1995), and Transport 2021, *The Cost of Transporting People in the British Columbia Lower Mainland* (Vancouver: 1993). True average driving speed assumes average driving distance from Litman, *Transportation Cost Analysis*. Median U.S. income for household of two from U.S. Bureau of the Census, *Statistical Abstract of the United States 1993* (D.C.: 1994). Average weekly driving time from John P. Robinson, "Americans on the Road," *American Demographics,* Sep. 1989. Infrastructure costs from James E. Frank, *Costs of Alternative Development Patterns* (D.C.: Urban Land Institute, 1989).

31. Todd Litman, "Internalizing and Marginalizing Parking Costs as a Transportation Demand Management Measure," VTPI, Victoria, 1995. Congestion from Dick Nelson and Don Shakow, "If We Spend Billions on

Regional Transportation, Shouldn't We Expect a Good Return on Our Investment?" Institute for Washington's Future, Seattle, 1995.

32. Economic loss estimated from National Safety Council, op. cit. note 3.

33. Farmland from Kathleen E. Moore, "Urbanization in the Lower Fraser Valley," Canadian Wildlife Service, Vancouver, 1990. Harm to economy from Bank of America et al., *Beyond Sprawl* (San Francisco: 1995).

34. Subsidies from John C. Ryan, *Hazardous Handouts* (Seattle: NEW, 1995). Tax effects from Roth, op. cit. note 8, and Sonoran Institute, "Fiscal and Economic Impacts of Local Conservation and Community Development Measures," Tucson, Ariz., 1993.

35. Federico Peña, Secretary, U.S. Dept. of Transportation, interview on National Public Radio, Dec. 15, 1995.

36. FHWA, *Highway Statistics* (D.C.: various editions), and Ministry of Transportation and Highways, Motor Vehicle Branch, *Traffic Accident Statistics* (Ottawa: various editions). Violent crime statistics from sources in note 3; and Howard N. Snyder and Melissa Sickmund, *Juvenile Offenders and Victims* (D.C.: U.S. Dept. of Justice, 1995).

37. Risks estimated 1995 crime statistics by census tract from Crime Prevention Office, Seattle Police Dept., unpublished data, Dec. 1995; on census-tract population data from PSRC, op. cit. note 14; suburban crime rates from King County, *1994 King County Annual Growth Report* (Seattle: 1994); Wash. injury-accident rate per mile from FHWA, op. cit. note 3; and urban-suburban driving rates from Holtzclaw, op. cit. note 9.

38. U.S. Advisory Board, op. cit. note 11. Delton W. Young, "Suburban Disconnect," *Seattle Post-Intelligencer*, Nov. 12, 1995, and Delton W. Young, "Suburbs No Escape from Youth Violence," *Seattle Post-Intelligencer*, Jul. 27, 1995.

39. Oil consumption estimated from B.C. Energy Council, op. cit. note 8; from Ore. Dept. of Energy, "Oregon Energy Statistics," Salem, January 1994, and from Idaho Dept. of Water Resources, *Idaho Energy Vital Statistics '94* (Boise: 1994). Oil defense from former Navy Secretary John F. Lehman, Jr., cited in Terry Sabonis-Chafee, "Oil Security and Hidden Costs" (letter), *Science,* Feb. 10, 1989.

40. Canada-Amsterdam comparison from William E. Rees and Mark Roseland, "Sustainable Communities," *Plan Canada,* May 1991. Comparison to other cities based on data in Table 1 and Ryan, op. cit. note 5.

41. Population-land development from Puget Sound Water Quality Authority, *State of the Sound: 1992 Report* (Olympia: 1992). Seattle land conversion from PSRC, *Vision 2020 Update: Environmental Impact Statement* (Seattle: 1994). Vancouver from Moore, op. cit. note 33.

42. Urban development on private rural land in U.S. Northwest from U.S. Dept. of Agriculture, Natural Resource Conservation Service (NRCS), published and unpublished data from National Resources Inventories of

1992, 1987, and 1982 provided to NEW by each state's NRCS office. Wetlands from Douglas J. Canning and Michelle Stevens, *Wetlands of Washington* (Olympia: Wash. Dept. of Ecology, 1990).

43. Schueler, op. cit. note 16.

44. Marcia D. Lowe, *Shaping Cities* (D.C.: Worldwatch Institute, 1991).

45. Effects of sprawl on poor and on urban neighborhoods from Litman, op. cit. note 30, Kunstler, op. cit. note 29. Neighborhood decay from Carnegie Corporation, op. cit. note 11.

46. American Association of Retired Persons, "Community Planning," AARP Policy Agenda, D.C., 1995.

47. Segregation of classes from Kunstler, op. cit. note 29, and Robert B. Reich, *The Work of Nations* (N.Y.: Knopf, 1991).

48. Time driving from Robinson, op. cit. note 30. Breakdown of community from Robert D. Putnam, "The Prosperous Community," *American Prospect*, spring 1993. Urban space estimated from sources in note 16 and Litman, op. cit. note 30.

49. Kunstler, op. cit. note 29.

50. Putnam, op. cit. note 47. Henry Richmond and Saunders C. Hillyer, "Need Assessment for a Metropolitan and Rural Land Institute," 1,000 Friends of Oregon, Portland, 1993.

51. Edwin Bender, research director, Money in Western Politics Project, Western States Center, unpublished data, Portland, May 1995.

52. Chapter draws on Kunstler, op. cit. note 29; Terry McDermott, "A Neighborhood Left Behind," *Seattle Times,* Dec. 13, 1992; Price, "Tale of Three Cities," op. cit. note 2; Carlos A. Schwantes, *The Pacific Northwest* (Lincoln: Univ. of Neb. Press, 1989); and Wynn and Oke, op. cit. note 20. Streetcar development from Sharon Boswell and Lorraine McConaghy, "On a Roll, City Spreads Out," *Seattle Times*, Feb. 25, 1996.

53. Figure 3 sources: U.S. vehicle registrations from FHWA, *Highway Statistics* (D.C.: various editions). B.C. from F. H. Leacy, ed., *Historical Statistics of Canada*, 2nd ed. (Ottawa: Statistics Canada, 1983), and Statistics Canada, *Road Motor Vehicle Registrations* (Ottawa: various editions).

54. Tax information from private communications with provincial and state tax authorities, and FHWA, *Highway Statistics 1994* (D.C.: 1995).

55. Kunstler, op. cit. note 29.

56. Redlining from McDermott, op. cit. note 52, and Penny Loeb et al., "The New Redlining," *U.S. News & World Report*, Apr. 17, 1995.

57. In-migration from Schwantes, op. cit. note 52. FHA from Kunstler, op. cit. note 29.

58. Peter Dreier and John Atlas, "The Scandal of Mansion Subsidies," *Dissent,* Winter 1992.

59. Kunstler, op. cit. note 29.

60. Kunstler, op. cit. note 29.

61. Walt Crowley, "Track to the Future," *Seattle Post-Intelligencer*, Mar. 5, 1995.

62. Interstates' effects from Price, "Tale of Three Cities," op. cit. note 2. Shopping malls from Alan Thein Durning, *How Much Is Enough?* (N.Y.: Norton, 1992).

63. Daniel Yergin, *The Prize* (N.Y.: Simon & Schuster, 1992).

64. Kunstler, op. cit. note 29. New shopping centers from Durning, op. cit. note 62. Savings and loan bail out from U.S. Congressional Budget Office, D.C., private communications, 1995.

65. Sport-utility vehicles from Agis Salpukas, "With Prices Low, Gasoline Guzzling Makes a Comeback," *New York Times*, Feb. 15, 1996. Parking spaces from Litman, op. cit. note 31. Roads from Ryan, op. cit. note 6.

66. Danny Westneat, "Late for the Train," *Seattle Times*, Mar. 5, 1995. Crowley, op. cit. note 61.

67. Portland from Kunstler, op. cit. note 29, Lowe, op. cit. note 44, and Philip Langdon, "How Portland Does It," *Atlantic Monthly*, Nov. 1992.

68. Earl Blumenaur, commissioner of public works, Portland, private communication, Dec. 9, 1994.

69. Langdon, op. cit. note 67.

70. Terry Moore, Metro Council, Portland, private communication, Dec. 10, 1994.

71. Preston Schiller, Alt-Trans, Kirkland, Wash., private communication, Nov. 16, 1994. Jonas Rabinovitch and Josef Leitman, "Urban Planning in Curitiba," *Scientific American*, Mar. 1996.

72. Lowe, op. cit. note 44.

73. Portland from Blumenaur, op. cit. note 68. Boise from Kim Eckart, "Mountains or Molehills," *Idaho Statesman*, Sep. 11, 1995.

74. Portland bicycles from Paul Wilson, "Changing Direction toward Sustainable Culture," *Northwest Report*, Jan. 1996.

75. Miles of freeway from Jeanne W. Wolfe, "Canada's Liveable Cities," *Social Policy*, summer 1992. Table 1: Shares of population in low-density neighborhoods from sources in note 14; other data from Schiller and Kenworthy, op. cit. note 18. Vancouver land conversion from Moore, op. cit. note 33. Seattle from sources cited in note 41.

76. Richmond and Hillyer, op. cit. note 50.

77. LUTRAQ from Bartholomew, op. cit. note 17, and LUTRAQ project, 1,000 Friends of Oregon, newsletters and reports, Portland, 1993–95.

78. Bartholomew, op. cit. note 17, LUTRAQ, op. cit. note 77.

79. Meeky Blizzard, Sensible Transportation Options for People, Tigard, Ore., private communication, Dec. 10, 1994.

80. Seattle sidewalks from Schiller and Kenworthy, op. cit. note 18.

81. LUTRAQ, op. cit. note 77.

82. Moore, op. cit. note 70.

83. Gussie McRoberts, mayor, Gresham, Ore., private communication, Dec. 10, 1994.

84. Todd Litman, VTPI, Victoria, private communication, Jun. 6, 1995.

85. Table 2 sources: Litman, op. cit. note 30.

86. Litman, op. cit. notes 30, 84.

87. Litman, op. cit. note 30.

88. Litman, op. cit. note 30.

89. Table 3: Gasoline consumption from Statistics Canada, *Road Motor Vehicles Fuel Sales 1994* (Ottawa: 1995), and FHWA, op. cit. note 54; vehicle travel per capita in B.C. estimated by NEW; net fuel tax is provincial-state and federal fuel tax on gasoline minus the estimated value of exemptions from state sales taxes, from FHWA, *Highway Statistics 1994*, private communications with state tax authorities for U.S. states, and Todd Litman, private communication for B.C.; average insurance premiums from Insurance Information Institute, *I.I.I. 1995 Fact Book*, cited in Todd Litman, "Marginalizing Insurance Costs As a Transportation Demand Management Measure," VTPI, Victoria, 1995.

90. Real fuel price from Yergin, op. cit. note 63.

91. Todd Litman, "Marginalizing Insurance Costs," op. cit. note 89.

92. Pay-at-the-pump insurance from Stephen D. Sugarman, *"Pay at the Pump" Auto Insurance* (Berkeley: Univ. of Calif., 1993), and Andrew Tobias, *Auto Insurance Alert!* (N.Y.: Fireside, 1993).

93. Litman, op. cit. note 31.

94. NEW surveyed Northwest cities' and counties' off-street parking requirements.

95. Portland from Schiller and Kenworthy, op. cit. note 18. Low-income housing from Litman, op. cit. note 30.

96. Donald Shoup, "An Opportunity to Reduce Minimum Parking Requirements," *Journal of the American Planning Association*, winter 1995.

97. "Bike Commuting to Downtown Grows," *Seattle Times*, Nov. 30, 1995.

98. Transit Department, *1994 Rider/Non-Rider Survey*, (Seattle: King County Dept. of Metropolitan Services, 1995).

99. WSEO, "Initial Impacts, Benefits, and Costs of Washington's Commute Trip Reduction Program," (Olympia: 1995). Employer programs from private communications with transportation coordinators at each corporation during early 1996, except Key Bank from Gene Mullins and Carolyn Mullins, "Proximate Commuting," Mullins & Associates, Seattle, 1995. Shortcomings of trip reduction programs from Genevieve Giuliano and Martin Wachs, "A Comparative Analysis of Regulatory and Market-Based Transportation Management Strategies," Univ. of Southern Calif., Los Angeles, 1992.

100. Litman, op. cit. note 31. Canadian law and enforcement from Ryan, op. cit. note 34. Vancouver parking from Transport 2021, op. cit. note 30. State tax policies from private communications with tax authorities and review of tax codes in each Northwest state.

101. Litman, op. cit. note 31, and "Marginalizing Insurance Costs," op. cit. note 89.

102. Thomas A. Gihring, "Converting from a Single Rate to a Differential Rate Property Tax," paper presented at Pacific Northwest Regional Economic Conference, Seattle, Apr. 28–30, 1994.

103. Clifford Cobb,"Fiscal Policy for a Sustainable California Economy" (draft), Redefining Progress, San Francisco, 1995.

104. Gihring, op. cit. note 102.

105. Cobb, op. cit. note 103. Eugene Levin,"Let the State of Washington . . . Look to the Land" (pamphlet, Common Ground U.S.A.), Seattle, March 1994.

106. Levin, op. cit. note 105, and Cobb, op. cit. note 103.

107. Cobb, op. cit. note 103. Levin, op. cit. note 103. Edward C. Baig,"Higher Taxes that Promote Development," *Fortune,* Aug. 8, 1983.

108. Assessment accuracy from each state and provincial tax authority.

109. International Association of Assessing Officers, *Assessment Administration Practices in the U.S. and Canada* (Chicago: 1992). B.C.'s stature from Gihring, op. cit. note 102, and B.C. Assessment Authority,"Real Property Taxation History and Principles," Victoria, 1995.

110. Discussion of shifting taxes draws on publications of Worldwatch Institute and World Resources Institute (WRI), both in D.C., since 1989, and on Cobb, op. cit. note 103; see Durning, op. cit. note 1.

111. Cobb, op. cit. note 103, and Roger C. Dower and Mary Beth Zimmerman, *The Right Climate for Carbon Taxes* (D.C.: WRI, 1992).

112. Vehicle-use pricing from ECO Northwest et al., *Evaluating Congestion Pricing Alternatives* (Seattle: PSRC, 1994).

113. Oregon Environmental Council, Portland, fact sheets, Feb. 1996.

114. FHWA, op. cit. note 54.

115. Amory B. Lovins and L. Hunter Lovins,"Reinventing the Wheels," *Atlantic Monthly,* Jan. 1995. Western Wash. Univ. from Rocky Mountain Institute, "Hypercars:Answers to Frequently Asked Questions," Snowmass, Colo., 1995.

116. Bikes from Nelson and Shakow, op. cit. note 31.

117. Vancouver growth from Price, op. cit. note 2. Workers from Ross Howard, "Greater Region May Be Misnomer," *Globe and Mail,* Dec. 9, 1994. Seattle growth plans from PSRC, op. cit. note 27. County plans from 1,000 Friends of Washington and U.W. Growth Management Planning and Research Clearinghouse, *Growth Management or Planned Urban Sprawl?* (Seattle: 1993).